Louis Menand

Autobiography and Recollections of Incidents Connected with

Horticultural Affairs, etc.

Louis Menand

Autobiography and Recollections of Incidents Connected with Horticultural Affairs, etc.

ISBN/EAN: 9783744678872

Printed in Europe, USA, Canada, Australia, Japan

Cover: Foto ©ninafisch / pixelio.de

More available books at **www.hansebooks.com**

AUTOBIOGRAPHY AND RECOLLECTIONS

OF INCIDENTS CONNECTED WITH

HORTICULTURAL AFFAIRS, ETC.

FROM 1807 UP TO THIS DAY 1892.

WITH PORTRAIT AND ALLEGORICAL FIGURES.

"By an ever practical wisdom seeker,"

L. MENAND.

WITH AN APPENDIX

OF RETROSPECTIVE INCIDENTS OMITTED OR FORGOTTEN IN THE ABOVE, MISCELLANEOUS, ETC.

ALBANY, N. Y.
WEED, PARSONS AND COMPANY.
1892.

Entered, according to act of Congress, in the year eighteen hundred and ninety-two,

By L. MENAND,

In the office of the Librarian of Congress, at Washington.

A PREFATORY HINT.

Before sending these little agglomerations of my recollections out of my hands, I feel, intuitively, I ought to make some remarks in relation to them, so as to save any one the trouble to make them for me, or against me, for, I am fully aware that some may possibly say that *recollector*, L. Menand, is passably endowed with *vanity* of all sorts, but especially *literary vanity* above all *poetical* vanity. These remarks, if made, are *perfectly right* and *natural*, according to our "human nature." Yet I want to apologize beforehand for that *venial* sin, *vanity*. "It ought to be wished" that all *sins* should be *similar* to mine in that *line, vanity in the highest degree*, and caused by the same *motives!* .... The community at large would not be *worse* if not *much better*....I have not much more to say to justify my *sin* or *sins*, for I *admit* I have more than one, though I do not monopolize them all. My *prose* and *poetry*, may be, are two of them, especially the *later*, for my justification I would say that I have never studied much the theory of either.

I have always written according to the dictates of my heart and conscience. Disregarding the *rules* (especially of poetry, of which I am perfectly ignorant, of the rules, but I *like* the *thing* when it has *common* sense, besides *rhymes — measured as with a rule*, as geographers do), but those of my own judgment being a "Homo asper" .... I will not say any more but that I am *more* or *less* like the rest of mankind.

Yours, etc.,
L. MENAND.

EXPLANATION.

To excuse our faults, often blunders, and occasionally *stupidity*, we, the sacred as the profanes, we quote the classic phrase:

"Quandoque bonus Homerus dormitat."—"Sometimes even the good Homer nods."

What I want to come at with this preliminary remark, is that *I*, who *am* apt to find "*atoms* in other people's eyes, I cannot see "*a Bœotian* monument" of stupidity in mine, *e. g*, last year I got an electrotyped species of cactus —— named "Anhalonium *fissuratum*, and I wrote the specific name *prismaticum*. A blind man could not see the difference of the plants, but could feel it, and yet it has taken me since a year,— and *seeing* the plant (*and name*) almost every day to discover my —— ? I cannot find a name adequate for that *idiotic* oversight and no chance to justify myself. I cannot say, as we often do, "It is my man's fault." This is no man's fault but a biped — but an ass!

Some, charitable people, will probably say: that old

man is *absent-minded!* but more may say: that enthusiast of good wine has absorbed too much.... whatever may be said I shall accept and I shall, I will laugh myself of my witticism, but my laugh is of an awful *blue* shade and not at all "*celestial!*" but the reverse. I hope for my comfort that my confession will be found sincere, in as much that I do not ask for absolution, I shall inflict myself an adequate penance if I live long enough.

I shall alter my *motto* and substitute another better appropriated, that will afterward legitimate any stupidities that come out of my head. *Here it is:* "Bœotûm in crasso jurares aëre natum." English: You would swear that he was born in the thick air of the *Bœotians,*—the people of the Greek province of Bœotia were proverbially remarkable for their stupidity.

L. MENAND.

AUTOBIOGRAPHY AND RECOLLECTIONS.

I have been told that I was born on the 2d of August, 1807, in the old province of France called Burgundy, a country noted for her good wine, probably one of the reasons I am more partial to wine than to whisky.

My father was a gardener and this somewhat accounts for my early love for horticulture. As far as I can recollect I was about eight or ten years old, more or less, when I began to try to grow plants from cuttings. I have always been fond of cutting! properly and figuratively speaking, except cutting my fingers! Besides, I was also very fond of reading books treating of gardening operations, especially the nomenclature — long names that I learned by heart, as parrots do, without knowing the meaning, which constitutes a poor learning. However, later in life I have found these words very useful. I found that "words lead to the knowledge of things." One thing I have never been able to learn is mathematics — I mean that lateral branch of it, "arithmetic," the science "par excellence." Even to-day, with more than three-quarters of a century of.... I cannot comprehend the mystery of the Trinity! Yet, I have always been able to count the money that has passed through my hands.

Excuse me this digression, and I return to my propagation that I continued to practice until I lost my father. Then I was between fifteen and sixteen years old, perhaps a little more, I cannot ascertain exactly. All that I am certain of is that I remained with my mother and sister until the month of March, 1827, when an idea — many ideas got into my head — that I was old enough to "think for myself" came to me, and that it would be serviceable to know the *sense* of all the words I knew by heart. One thing I knew by experience — the culminating one — that the steeple of my city (Châlons-sur-Saone, Dept. de Saone-et-Loire, France) did not afford me shade or protection enough, or rather too much of it, for I foresaw that ultimately it would "etiolate" my conceptions in the bud! Then I at once came to the conclusion to leave my Penates, my Lares and my other household gods and move to the "capital of the civilized world"— according to the general idea of the French, but not exactly to mine — which was and still is cosmopolitan.

Paris, then, for me was an "Eldorado" where I thought, in my puerile innocence, that every one was, or ought to be, a philosopher!....or something of that sort. Ah! what a philosophy!! you will soon see. In a few days after I had decided to leave my home I was in Paris, in company with a philosopher! I got acquainted with in the stage-coach, who kindly offered me his services, as he supposed I would not know where to go at such time of night — 10 or 11 P. M. When we got out of the stage he hired a cab and told me he was going to carry me to his *hotel!* Before getting into the cab the first sight I had of Paris was such a fog as I had never seen before and never have since. The Parisians called it London fog. I think I could have cut a slice off it. In a few minutes we reached that hotel! located in a narrow, gloomy, dirty street in the "city" — the old Paris — within a few hundred yards of Notre Dame, that church so graphically delineated by Victor Hugo, in his wonderful book "Notre Dame de Paris." That hotel looked to me paltry, dirty, cutthroat, etc., etc. That *den* a few years later became famous from having been the spot where the social —— romancer, "Eugene Sue," introduced his hero and heroine, Prince Rodolphe and Fleur de Marie, in his marvellous book, "Les Mysteres de Paris." I took supper that night and in the morning breakfast bought from a restaurant, with my "cicerone," and never saw him again but six months after by chance in the "Champs Elysées." He made an apology for not having *warned* me of what I would see in that Hotel *du Diable*. Notwithstanding his living in such atmosphere that man was an honest man, for it was on his recommendations, etc., that nothing bad had happened to me. I slept three nights there. In the day time I ran through the city to deliver some letters of recommendation, etc. During those three evenings and nights I learned more than I did thereafter in ten years.

The same day I left that vestibule of hell I went to take possession of a situation as an assistant gardener in one of the most aristocratic suburbs of Paris, with a different breed of philosophers. There I was somewhat in my dreamed-for element. Many green and hothouses full of rare plants ; few of them I knew, except the *names* of some ; but I could not apply the names to the plants, and when I attempted to ask the names of the head gardener — a sort of biped bear! he answered me : " You had better to mind your work, for if you have any ambition to be a gentleman's gardener you will do better to learn forcing vegetables," etc., etc. To that hint I replied that I thought it would be better to work for the people who carried on that business, and as I was among plants I wished to know something about them ; that gentlemen who wanted forced vegetables wanted also plants, etc. He stared at me with a frown and told me to go to my work — pointing with his hand to a certain hothouse; "there you will find that large plant in a tub, that has leaves the shape of a *gardener's trowel!*".... was not that description a philosophic circumlocution to avoid telling me the name of it? Inwardly — in my sleeves — I laughed, for I knew the plant and its name. So, as I was in contact with philosophers, I durst, I had the temerity to speak with my mouth open and with my heart also. I humbly replied: "I do not know exactly if I understand rightly; your description is somewhat novel to me and very picturesque. I think you mean the Strelitzia reginæ!" " Who told you that, *Mr. The Doctor?*" he responded, with a sneer that had a heinous look. From that I had won the sympathy of that charming man. Truly, there was no love lost between us. I liberally reciprocated his sentiments toward me. I had been recommended to him by one of his acquaintances to whom I think he was under obligations, and he did not like to say he did not want me, for he was looking for a man. I thought that he hated me the first time he spoke to me.

When I went in that place I had some *local expressions* that were not very exactly the purest French, and I knew it; but the habit was sticking to me. However, I soon got rid of them — quicker than he had

learned French orthography. A few days after the
coining of that description of a leaf "like a gardener's
trowel," he gave me a chance to retaliate. We were
potting some carnations. A young man, with me,
were potting, and *he*, the "neologist in *description*,
was writing the labels, and threw them to us on the
floor where we were potting, bent on our knees — no
potting bench. I supposed it was for the purpose of
doing penance — it was in Lent time ! (I feel that I
am overstretching.) I caught a label spelt wrong, and
as it was only a few moments since he had laughed at
me, I thought the occasion was a good one to reciprocate, so I told him that name was incorrect — in my
village we spelt it with a double r. "You think so,
Mr. The Doctor ! " " I do not *think*, I am *sure* of
it ! " On that affirmation he started like a runaway
horse. The young man with me asked what was the
matter with the boss. I told him, "I think he has
gone to his room to look in his dictionary to see if I
am right." What, right? that young philosopher somewhat belonged to the school of our boss, and thought
it childish to get mad for one letter more or less, but
he was a philosopher of the *sect of the quiets*, and did
not trouble himself any more about the incident. From
that time our boss did not make any more jokes on my
local expressions, but did not like me any better. I
remained under his sway about eighteen months, till

August, 1828. Before leaving that *Neologist* I must sketch some of his features: That man was typical, even in his name — *David*. I have never known his initials. He was always called *David*. As you would say: God! or his antithesis, the *Devil*. At that time his facial look suggested to me that he was an Israelite, but not born in Bethlehem. He was a *Normand* from Rouen, Normandy. Seen *in profile*, his face somewhat looked, *to me*, like the upper end of a carving knife with some indentations simulating his mouth, his nose, etc. This last nasal appendix was very remarkable. It was aquiline like the beak of the eagle in appearance, but to my *fancy* I thought he looked in his mind, always for me, like a compound of a goose, or a hawk, or an owl, or like any nocturnal animal of prey.

It is only since I have seen the portrait of "Fagin, in Oliver Twist," that I have realized he might have been a descendant, direct or indirect of that character, Fagin, but it matters not this moment. After *sixty-four years* I have the profound conviction that the *David* of my heart and *Fagin*, must have been identical — morally and physically speaking. Only my David had some resemblance to the King of Israel. In one respect *my David* had to my knowledge *seduced* or *bought* another man's wife, but I do not think he killed the husband, so there was a little *less* criminality in my type than in our *King*, but for some persons *a King* can commit ADULTERY, A CRIME, and not be a *criminal* as a common *mortal*, for, according to some *casuists, what* his *crime* with one is *virtue*, with another, especially *when* that *manKing* or *not* has written some *religious poetry*.............. I think I have done with my digressions of my "*never forgotten Neologist.*" The *chords* of my *soul* he had touched with his irrational hatred are still vibrating!!............ This closed the first act of my debut in life. Then I changed, in one way for the worse, but every day adding something to my theories of life.

I shall pass over all my tribulations during the year 1829, the most unlucky and inauspicious of my life, so much so as willing to be gone *ad patres*. At the close of that year I had the good luck to find a situation where I found a library at my disposal. I fell on one work by Lamarck and Decandolle, " La Flore Francaise," which work *revolutionized* the course of my ideas and opened a new field to my ambition for new studies, a study not exactly connected to horticulture, but which absorbed me at once — the study of " wild plants," if that expression is proper, and especially " Cryptogamous plants." Every one who knew me, when I told them my discovery of that book, laughed at me, and said, in plain language, that

I was a *down right fool.* I admitted the epithet, but did not change my mind. What a stupid idea, will say my acquaintances *of to-day*, to study "cryptogamy" to be a florist; "it is absurd!" Be it so, but paradoxical as it may be, it has been more beneficial to me than growing coleus at seventy-five cents per 100 !! It has in the first place given me *self gratification!* It has systematized my ideas, in theory and in practice. It has brought me in contact with people that would otherwise never have looked at me. When later I made up my mind to cultivate exotic plants, such as Ericas, Banksias, and all kinds of New Holland plants, I was saluted with the same reverence — I was a fool! such business would not pay, etc., etc.

But I perceive that I am overflowing on my subject. I am anticipating upon the future by fifty years. So I return to the first reading of my *French Flora*, and the cryptogamic ideas it wove in my brain! Cryptogamic indeed! since they were not understood. In the beginning of 1830 I had to leave my library and its books to settle a short distance further, but always in the precincts of Paris. It was my third year of gravitation around that luminous terrestrial planet, that was soon to be more luminous by kindling that "Three days' revolution!" Revolution that I wished and expected since two or three years, at the time I laid down the plan — the foundation — of my religious and political creed, with that aphorism: "No kings! No Medium between Man and Heaven; every one his own arbitrator, free will! in spiritual affairs."

That year, 1830 to April, 1831, closed what I would call the *first phase* of my life. Then I left Paris and went to take possession of a situation as a gardener in the province "Champagne," the classical land of the wine so-called, where I lived over six years, the quietest period of my life. There I could study without being sneered at, but on the contrary I was encouraged to do so. But, alas! as before, I could not understand the meaning of Latin and Greek names of plants, and at that time we had not such a valuable work as Mr. Nicholson's "Dictionary of Gardening." Somewhat as by intuition I understood or *guessed* that such adjectives as grandiflorus, grandiflora and grandiflorum meant large flowers, but I was perplexed about the termination in *us*, *a* and *um*. How I sighed at my ignorance, and no way, I thought, to learn, for I was as most young men were, and still are to-day. If you have not received a collegiate education when young, you can never get it after, especially when you are deprived of means. Notwithstanding that drawback I felt that I could do something. I was determined to try. One day I heard of a certain gentleman — a notary public, who was managing the financial affairs of my employer (an old lady) — who was a *good* Latinist. He was not, but he put me in the way of doing something to enlighten me on the subject. So the first time he came to the place I watched for him and introduced myself. With a book in my hand I told him what I had heard of his knowledge, etc., etc. He sharply looked at me and said: "What do you want of me?" I showed him my adjectives in us, a, um, etc., and I told him I thought they meant so and so. He looked at me between my two eyes and gravely told me: "If you know that why do you ask me?" I answered that I thought I knew but was not certain, but what I know not are those terminations, etc. "Those terminations," he said, "are masculine, feminine and neuter, and if you know as much as you evidently seem to, get a Latin grammar, and in a few days you will know as much as I do." "To get a Latin grammar I shall have to go twelve miles to get it" (we were in the country). "I know it," he said, "but to-morrow I go thither (to Rheims, the next city) and I shall bring you one." I made the remark that a grammar would not give me all the information I wanted. "I must have a dictionary of French and Latin and Latin and French." My employer — who was present — said: "Bring him also those dictionaries," etc. He put his hands on my shoulders and said: "Young man, if you have *guessed* all that you have told me, you will go far, and when you have looked over your grammar for a few days, come and see me at my office, to show me your progress in *guessing* Latin." I went to see him two or three weeks after, and I found that if he was not a good Latinist he was a *good man*, and he gave me good advice. He kept me two or three hours, talking politics, theology, literature, etc.

I will continue my course for a little while longer on the European continent; then I shall sail for the western hemisphere, my adoptive country, where I have *lived happy!!* for fifty-four years, less a fortnight, when *dark clouds* suddenly *eclipsed* forever *my sunshine! half of my life* — my Egeria! my wife.... You will please excuse the above extemporaneous digression. I could not refrain doing it. It choked me....

I resume the narration of my studies. I was in possession of the instruments, books, to elucidate the meaning of words stuffed in my head. The first night I got that grammar I did not sleep much. I spent most part of it to decline the first declension : penna, pennæ or rosa, rosæ, etc., and went to bed reciting:

Nominative rosa;
Genitive, rosæ;
Dative, rosæ;
Accusative, rosam;
Vocative, o rosa;
Ablative, rosa.

Here I decline rosa! as a compliment to our friends, the rose growers

When I say I did not sleep much, to tell the truth I don't think I slept at all, for I think I was still humming "Nominative rosa" when I opened my eyes and saw the light, or, rather, the dawn of day, as the dawn of my motions, dusky! It was a Sunday morning in June, and I intended to go herborizing; so I got up, took up my herborizing box and started across meadows, woods, swamps, etc. I had walked a considerable distance, when I found myself on an eminence, wet above the knees by the dew, and not feeling too comfortable, when I turned round and I saw the rays of the sun emerging out of the horizon. I was dazzled by the sublime magnificence of that *Light God!!* that *supreme unknown!!* For awhile I forgot my grammar, the cryptogamous and phanerogamous plants. The whole nature, the creation, which I was contemplating with so much admiration that all my moral, intellectual faculties were.... I could not analyze them, was so bewildered it took some time before I could realize where I was, my blood still in ebullition and my legs cold, but it did not last long. That *God-Light* soon warmed me again, and when I got over my ecstacy I began to realize I had often seen a rising of the sun, but never in such a circumstance. So I immediately resumed my search for a certain plant, of which I scented the smell before I saw it. I was trampling it under my feet; it was an orchideæ, "Satyrium hircinum," a well-baptized plant, from its horrid he-goat's smell. This is another digression — perhaps out of place — but it is an incident of my life and I "sketch it!" And I have many more incidental episodes to relate, but I shall pass them over, or most of them.

I went on with my studies of Latin and cryptogamy and a few other odd ideas, notions, etc. I progressed moderately well. The first use I made of my embryonic knowledge of Latin was quite a diminutive triumph for my vanity. I can not refrain from recounting it.

I had a young man working with me who was going to marry. One day he asked me if he could not have half a day to go and see his betrothed. I told him he could, but I told him jokingly: "My dear fellow, if you marry before the priest you will have to go to confess, if not he will not marry you ; but if you give up the religious ceremony and get satisfied to be married before your mayor or any other official, all right! As the French law does not recognize the religious ceremony as legal, you can choose." He answered me that he would not go to confess and would get married! "Well, do as you please," I responded. When he came to work the following day he showed me a sheet of paper folded in four parts, not sealed, nor any envelope at that time. It was a certificate about his morality. No, I forget now, but at the bottom of that document there was a postscript in Latin that he could not understand — the reason I suppose that he showed it to me. That postscript was to inform the priest who would marry him that he (the one who had written it) had not heard the confession of the bearer. It was short: "Domine, Non audivi confessionem, Johan...." etc. I cannot remember names. After reading it I told him "You have not been to confess." "How do you know?" he replied, looking at me with a change in his countenance, turning pale as if he had committed a crime. "Well, I know it. Do you not know that heretics, free thinkers and 'bloody Republicans' — as they called me — as they called us — can guess a good many things? Besides, this paper tells me that you have not." "What shall I do?" he asked in a tremulous voice. By that time I had returned his paper. "Give it to me again; I will fix it all right." I folded the bottom of the paper containing the P. S., cut it off and handed him both the certificate and the P. S. and told him, "Now you can do what you please; give both to the priest or only one, and he will marry you if you care for the religious ceremony. If not, get the mayor of your village, and he will marry you, and that is the only legal marriage according to French law. He got married, but I never heard anything about the particulars, the conclusions, nor did I care; I had the fun, that's all I wanted.

From this stage of my condition in that place, until June, 1837, I have not many incidents of my life to relate, besides what I said before, only that new ideas added to old ones, were constantly fomenting in my brain, owing to my solitary life, for I had nobody with whom I could exchange my views, my conceptions, except some occasional correspondence with acquaintances in Paris. The revolution of 1830 had disappointed me; from that event I had expected the proclamation of the Republic, laws more liberal, universal suffrage; instead of that, and thanks to the influence of General Lafayette and other lukewarm Republicans of the same school, we had another King. The political and religious constitution did not suit me, and every day I was sighing for the moment I would have money enough to quit France. I tried to get a situation under the government to go to Madagascar, but the man who could get me the position would not do it; he had been there two or three years and had been sick all the time, etc., etc. "I am sorry." "I, too," he said, "though you are one of those d—— exalted Republicans who frequently compel us National Guards to take our muskets to quell your stupid notions of Democracy," etc. He was a good man enough but he was gangrened

with royalism — more royalist than the king; one
of those philosophers of the school of the *stagnants!*
His ideas were flowing only when he was at the head
of his company of the militia to hunt the Republicans,
whom, I must say, were not all saints, far from it; but
brutal force is a poor way of civilizing men. Under
Louis Phillippe *emeutes* (*mobs*) were of daily occurrence.

All these things did not help me to cherish my
native country, inasmuch as I had already adopted that
device: "Ubi Libertas ibi patria " — " Where liberty
dwells, there is my country ;" and that country I contemplated should be the United States of North America. With all such reflections maturing in my mind,
I determined to move onward ; so immediately I made
my preparations to leave my situation, and in a few
weeks I was in Paris on my way to Havre. Before
leaving Paris I stopped with a friend for a few days,
during which he took me to the "Sorbonne," one of
the oldest universities in he world, to attend a lecture
on botany by the LAST of the *Jussieu* (Adrien de Jussieu), a family of savants. While there I met a great
many young students, lawyers, physicians and other
philosophers in embryo, who, when they understood I
was going to America, flocked around me and asked
me, without any ceremony, if I would send them spec-

imens of American plants for their herbaria. I replied in the same tune, that I was just going to cross the Atlantic to collect them, etc. One of them, especially, clung to me, with a specimen plant the professor was to lecture on, and asked me if I would tell him the name! To that question I asked him how long he had been attending the lectures. He replied "two or three years." "*Three years!* and you do not know that plant that grows on the old wall of your father's garden?" It was Linaria cymbalaria, and in three years he had not been able to know that plant. After the lecture was over I asked my friend if there were many students of the same stamp as the one who had asked me the name of a plant growing with him. "No," he said, "not perhaps over two-thirds!!" We went off making comments on the young "savants" we had just left. All of them had received a *college education*.

On the last day of July, 1837, I left Paris for Havre, whence I sailed for New York, where I landed on the 7th of September, 1837.

Then I was on *free! land* — with *slaves* not far off, held in bondage by another class of philosophers, of the school of the "Roman patricians," who, like Brutus, who stabbed his father, Cæsar, because he was a tyrant, and he at the same time compelled his slaves to fight against wild beasts in the arenas for his distraction. Here allow me a short digression. I have omitted above, that before landing and passing at the custom house, a countryman of mine, a *sort* of lawyer, asked me: " When the custom-house officers will ask you ' what is your profession ? ' what will you answer ? " " Of course I will answer that I am a gardener," I replied. " You are a fool if you do that," said he. " Why do you not say that you are a *botanist ?*" I could not help laughing, and answered him, " I suppose I am a botanist as much as you are a lawyer ; probably better, for I know a cabbage from a lettuce, and you — you do not know the difference between a *lawyer* and a *liar!* which for me are often synonymous expressions." When we passed the inspector he was first. He said he was a lawyer ! They laughed for a few seconds, then they asked me, " Are you a lawyer too ?" " No, I am a gardener." " Good ! " said one of the inspectors in French, " you have a better chance to find employment than your friend." He was not my friend. He tried to be, but in vain ; he got my contempt.

I was in New York, but I had very little money. As a compensation I had quantities of letters of recommendation to people in New York, Philadelphia, Washington, New Orleans and Havana. In this last city I had almost the certitude of a situation as curator of a botanic garden under the governorship of General Tacon, but my desire to learn English made me give up all the recommendations except those for New York, one for Dr. Torrey and one for Mr. George Thorburn. In a few days I had employment with the latter at Astoria, L. I., then "Hallett's Cove." It was only a year or two later that that village was named Astoria, from J. Jacob Astor, who had given $10,000 for the *christening*, etc. There I began to work my salvation, material and spiritual, digging up of the ground to plant trees and shrubs, and the English grammar, to find the "roots of all evils." I have found some, but have worn out many spades before I could rest on the laurels that I have cultivated for fifty-four years. It is in Astoria that I found the greatest number of the cryptogamous plants which I have sent to France. It was at Astoria, also, that I found the best specimen of the animal kingdom's production, "*a Phanerogyne!!*"* whom I have lost in 1890.... That Phancrogyne was not indigenous to Astoria, but was a British production, of British and French blood. This plant I have cultivated for fifty years, less a fortnight. When I saw it for the first time I was somewhat puzzled, but in a very short time I found I had discovered a typical form of vegetation and felt wonderfully anxious to have it in my herbarium. But it was not an ordinary speci-

---

* $\Phi a\nu \epsilon \rho o\varsigma$ $\Gamma \upsilon \nu \eta$. Phaneros Guné. Hence Phanerogyne, Phaneros — manifest, visible. Guné — woman, wife, etc.

men of vegetation that one can put between two sheets of paper and dry it. Nevertheless it took me over two months, and a considerable number of sheets of paper and ink, with all the quintessence of my rhetoric, before I could *press* it. Many will think I knew something about it before my finding. No! nothing at all. Not even its vernacular name; and in less than two hours after my discovery of this *rara avis* it had flown toward the north pole, Albany. When I heard of that flight I thought I had been mystified, and yet I thought I had been able to read the inner nature of my plant. So I had. I found it thereafter, to my jubilation. But since...... Oh, Phanerogyne!! *of half of my life*, of my soul! once more! adieu! adieu forever! adieu pour toujours! Vale æternum!!....
....Here ends the second phase of my life.

On the 30th of October, 1840, I started for Albany, following the track of my plant, my rara avis, or my phanerogyne as you please. For me these three appellations suit me. On the 31st of October I got fast bound in the chains of marriage. Then on the same day we left Albany on the steamboat, where, for the beginning of my honeymoon we had to separate — to divorce. There were no state rooms yet. Ladies stopped on the upper deck and men had to go down. When, in the morning we arrived at New York, Mr.

Thorburn, my employer, was waiting for us, and taking both of us by the hands, and in a loud thrilling voice, addressed me so : "Now my dear fellow!! you will have to stay at my house as I had proposed to you when you went, and you said you would not, and would go straight to Astoria. You may go if you please, but your house is burned to the ground," and he laughed. "It was burned before you were half way to Albany." I did not believe him; I thought he was joking. "Well," he said, "if you doubt, go and see it, but leave your bird here at my house. She will not fly out of the cage." So I started at once, and when I arrived I saw a nice heap of ashes on the site of the house. Everything had been burned except my bedstead, a table and a few other things. My bed room stood north and the fire had been *set* on the south with a north wind, so that a carpenter who had been building a greenhouse for us, and who knew I was in Albany, and living close by, when going to bed saw the house on fire and he ran at once for my room, broke the window, for the entrance of the house was already burned, and saved the few articles mentioned. The most important article was a table — a lucky table — in which I had $300 in gold in a purse. It had been thrown in a bed of roses, where I found it, the legs up. At once it struck me that the purse was gone, for the drawer was not locked. I went to it, opened the drawer, and saw my purse with contents intact. I had had $500 in it, but had taken $200 to go to be "chained."

From November 1840 until March 1842, I continued to conduct Mr. Thorburn's business at Astoria. Then we parted and I came to Albany to try my chance as a florist and nurseryman. I located on the Albany and Troy road, on a modest scale — more than modest, i. e. *meagre!* Do you wish to have a slight idea of it? Well! before the year 1842 was over every cent of the five or six hundred dollars, or a little over, were gone, and in nine months, from March to December, business was so *prosperous* that during that lapse of time I received $17! We spent at least $100 a month. Had it not been for that Phanerogyne, that Egeria of mine, I would have had to bundle up, to bundle off, for climes more hospitable, but that diminutive (in appearance), that *rara avis*, that bird of mine, saved us from a complete wreck. Not only saved us, but upheld my courage, and when the rose buds or buds of any description, failed to open, she supplied them with *musical notes!* Now! you will understand my love, my devotion, my veneration for that *personified providence.* She never flinched; her fortitude upheld her will! and in my eyes the exiguity of her stature transfigured her as a "giantess!!"

However, the year 1843 began under a more auspicious sky. We had had hard times. From that day we went *"pianissimo,"* but we never retrograded. Some "cryptogamic" ties held us, held us to our determination to swim or sink together, and we did so for fifty years. We swam in a lake of bliss!! That lake had become an ocean when a cyclone rent our blessedness! forever - - - - . The years 1843, '44, 45' and '46 passed off with very little progress, except in the double line of propagation — in the vegetable and the animal kingdoms. But we had got possession of a better and cheaper location, 300 or 400 yards from where we were, we had purchased four acres of land, built a house, etc., where we moved on the 1st of April, 1847. We were proprietors (in parte) and we were on the way to improvement. Plenty of elbow room to apply my device "Help thyself and God will help thee," and I was cheerfully willing to put the theory into practice — to work, work more and to pray together. As I have said above, our double line of propagation required more energy on my part, as my helpmate could not much longer substitute musical notes for the missing rose buds. I could sufficiently (with elbow and brain oil) do it myself.

At that juncture a slight fever broke out among the community of Albany and Troy for hardy perennial plants, and as I had a fair collection I did well; for three or four years, in the spring I was for a few weeks busy in putting up collections of 6 or 12 or more; also a few shrubs. When that fever subsided the fever for conifers, arbor vitæs and Norway spruces, balsam firs, etc., took its place, but with better remuneration ten fold, and the fever lasted longer, and in after years I had specimens of Siberian arbor vitæs for my own gratification that I sold for $20 each; of smaller ones I sold more than I could grow, for $2 and $2.50, including planting and warranting to live; if they did not live I replaced, or no pay! It was at that time I began to hear that often silly expression: "It won't pay to warrant trees to live." I have done it for 25 years or more and it has always paid me handsomely. And yet I had to compete with parties who sold as good looking trees as mine for 75 cents and $1 when I asked $2 and over. I transplanted our trees every other year when not every year. I followed the same practice for dwarf pear trees, then so popular. I think I have said somewhere that I had no faculty for learning arithmetic, yet I have always understood that the straight line was the shortest in geometry as in commercial transactions.

The above digressions have made me forget our propagations, which were going "*crescendo*" in both

lines. Then horticulture was progressing forward — not backward as I have seen in many instances on the fallacious pretext that it "did not pay." Then you could sell New Holland and Cape of Good Hope plants, etc., that nobody wants to-day. I think I shall do well not to follow the thread of my digressions on that subject when the "Chrysanthomania" is at the apogee of its paroxysm. Fifty years ago the camellia swayed! the horticultural world as the chrysanthemum does to-day. Everything has to undergo the vicissitudes of life, "Hodie mihi, cras tibi," to-day to me to-morrow to you. Among the various epidemics on plants we have had in succession are the "Morus multicaulis," "Chinese Yam" (Dioscorea), Fuchsia, Coleus, Pelargonium zonale and P. inguinans, vulgo geranium (horse shoe — geraniums), which by the way are *not* geraniums, notwithstanding the popularity of the name adapted by the whole community. We must confess that nothing has equalled *the rose!* which has survived and thrown into oblivion all her contemporaries. Roses were in demand 50, 60, 100 years ago. Not so much as to-day, however. Now they seem to be as necessary as bread itself! I wonder if they shall ever have their decadence? Do not be afraid. I only ask the question. It is not probable that the rose will ever be supplanted by any other flower — unless.....
God knows! we don't! One thing I know just this

moment. It is that I am sketching my life!? I hope it will be considered so! But I can not refrain from making digressions — right or wrong.

Well, I can not stop here, I must continue my wandering reflections. I think we are about the year 1850 or 1852; really I forget, but one year more or less will not make me one day older, even if I commit some anachronism, as long as what I relate is correct, and I earnestly mean to do so, or my quotation about straight and "short line" would be a fiction, a blunder, a falsehood. On second thought I think that what I am to tell happened in 1852 (but I am not certain and I have no documents to confirm my doubts), an attempt to revive the New York Horticultural Society, which had been founded several years before, (from what I had learned from Dr. Torrey, who certainly told me the year, but after more than half a century I forget) by having an exhibition. Messrs. Hogg, florists at Yorkville, hinted to me something about it and said, "when we have it we expect your presence, you can be represented. We understand you have materials for." I replied jocosely, "I shall not do such things. I would be afraid of distancing you in the contest and that might check the growth of our friendship." Time passed away and I had forgotten the incident, when one day I received a formal invitation to attend the exhibition. I did not intend to do it, but when the day came, my wife — No! my *Phanerogyne* — this name suits me; it is more sympathetic, more euphonic to me. Because it is Greek and of your own coining, you will say. No! it is not that; mother and father· are not entirely Greek and yet I somewhat like these expressions better than the equivalents of my maternal tongue, *mère* and *père*. It seems to me there is more sentiment in the English my mother! my father! are so full of euphony, of fluidity from the heart! I hope you will absolve me once more for that overstretched parenthesis. It was necessary to let you know my feelings! My Phanerogyne I was saying, was with me when Messrs. Hogg hinted to me the possibility of an exhibition and heard my jocose answer. She asked me are you not going to that exhibition? I answered no, I have too much to do, besides I have nothing in bloom, and no foliage plants — as to-day, no palms. "Well," said she, "if you do not go they will say that you are a vain boaster, with your fears of distancing them, etc. You ought to go. If it is only for my sake, do go!" I answered, "well I will, but without plants." "But it is precisely the plants which must go. They can do without you, but they want to see your plants." "Well, to please you I will try." So I went to look over my stock, which was not quite so large as that of Messrs. Pitcher & Manda to-day. I had only several Ixora coccinea in bloom and one Euphorbia splendens. I forget what were the other plants. I wanted six. I took two Ixoras — if not three. At that time I had never seen an exhibition, but I was reading the *Gardeners' Chronicle* and I knew the theory of the arrangements for exhibitions, and my *two* or *three* Ixoras forbade me of being disqualified from competition. I knew that the plants were to be dissimilar. However, I took the first prize for 6 plants — the prize of honor — notwithstanding the duplicate ixoras, but they were fine and had never been seen in New York. So I at once became a hero! Not one of Homer's heroes, though I drank water with my wine as they did; that was my only affinity with them.

That exhibition was, according to what I heard at the time, the most remunerative, they ever had in New York; but the receiver or treasurer forgot to give up the money received and ran away. And that "*Dutchman* from Albany," as I heard some people designating me, came back home covered with *platonic* laurels! But then, I could *fan* myself with...... I won't tell. If you are sagacious, as I suppose you are, you may guess at it.

As a bisextile year I am going to *leap* over to February 14, 1854, to receive a communication from a committee of gentlemen, lovers of horticulture, of

Brooklyn, asking me to let them have a copy of the by-laws of our horticultural society of Albany, and soliciting also my co-operation toward organizing or reviving their horticultural society. The New York Horticultural Society was then in a state of *catalepsy*, that with time became a chronic disease, with intermissions of a quasi life, just enough to show it was not dead. I with enthusiasm sent them the documents wanted and the promise of my co-operation as far as I could, and as I was wont to, I made the remark that I wished them success, that they had materials for but that they must try to control the "*element-gardener*" and prevent them from predominating their position, not let them transgress, trespass its limits. I then thought of a fair exhibition that took place in 1840, in Brooklyn, which never had an echo until May, 1854. From that year until 1861 all the exhibitions — two or three every year — were successful, partly thanks to the president, Mr. Degraw, a very liberal man, ready to put his hand in his pocket when the funds were short. It was at those exhibitions in Brooklyn that were seen the handsomest specimens of New Holland and Cape of Good Hope plants ever exhibited in America, besides many other plants such as Ixoras coccinea, javanica, Colei (white), etc., etc. I do not remember all, except some fine plants, much appreciated then, that would make people laugh to-day, not because they were inferior, but because they were *old!* As far as I can remember I attended most, if not all, of those exhibitions from 1854 to 1861, when the secession war put an end to the society's life. It expired in the Academy of Music of Brooklyn. I have said that the breaking out of the war put an end to it; but even if it had not, there would have been a catastrophe. The "element" alluded to had transgressed, trespassed over the limits of sound judgment. First by passing a resolution that "foreign exhibitors" should not have the freight of their exhibits paid, even if the freight should cost more than all the prize money they might receive. Now, do you understand who were those foreign exhibitors? You do not! Well, those foreign intruders were your correspondent, the "sketcher" of the above bitter-sweet digressions, etc. Secundo: that fifth element had decided *sub-rosa* not to award any first premiums to that Albany intruder who durst accept money to pay his freight, a mere trifle of $35 or $45 or more at every exhibition. One point to their credit, they did not deny me the right to vote at the presidential election. You may possibly wish to know who gave me such information. Simply the president of the society and its other officers, who had warned me not to mind the "elements quaking," that every thing should remain in the "statu quo" as before.

From that time the community at large seemed more inclined to *win* laurels than to *cultivate* them and I think they were right in that occurrence. The *abolition* of *slavery* was *more glorious* than all the exhibitions put together. "That Holy War!" "Cette Guerre Sainte" "Hoc Bellum Sanctum!" which has elevated the supremacy of the Anglo-American race, *Americano-Yankee progeny!*" This last appellation suits me better; in it I feel the pulsation of the shaking of the hand of *our Uncle Sam!* sez he!! The supremacy of that sublime *monotype* nation! I say monotype emphatically — for which other nation on the whole surface of the globe after the victory of the federal armies over the *old prejudices* would have used such clemency, behaved so generously with the vanquished??? None! Unless that *magnanimous?* Russia that would have done something that *Yankees!* would not have done, to-wit: hang half of the vanquished and send the other in Siberia for life........

That war which has elevated the supremacy, the glory of the grandest Republic in the world to the highest altitude; exalted the bravery of that *improvised army!!* that many *pygmies! mentally* speaking, said was fond of playing "*soldiers.*" *Indeed!* they were fond of playing, so fond of it that in 1865 *our Uncle Sam!* to make them give up the *idea* of continuing the *play* with that "*Scoundrel III, Third,*" had to intimate to the French army in Mexico to evacuate that country, that the *soil* the *spot* was too *hot* for their comfort, and that the sooner they would leave the better. He (our uncle) was not obliged to *re-intimate* the *hint;* it was readily understood, as by *intuition* and complied with *double quick* alacrity............

My commentaries on the resolutions of the "*fifth element*........" and on the war, have distracted me from my subject — the Exhibition. I do not remember well, but I think it was inferior to previous ones. The most attractive, strikingly so, was a lot of *Coleus Verschaffettii*, exhibited for the *first time*, by Mr. — I do not know the initials — Townsend of Brooklyn. The plants were *well grown!* and their brilliancy was *dazzling*, at least they produced that effect on me. As I drew near them I took off my hat out of admiration and *sighed deeply* with *eager desire* to get some of them, or at least some cuttings. I did not know the owner or else I would have introduced myself to him as a "professor of *cutting*" and ready to give him a demonstration of my skill in *vegetable anatomy*, but he was not in the Hall and I never saw him. And yet I got the cuttings on the same day! How? you will know soon. Having seen all I wanted to see I left the Exhibition room, I mean the Academy of Music, that I had seen for the first time and the last. Then I went to New York, to see the secretary of our Horticultural Society to get some information. I was hardly in his office when I saw a branch of our *Coleus!* before I saw him, standing in a glass of water on his desk. I went to the desk took the glass in my hand and presenting it to him I asked him where he took it, or *hooked* it perhaps I forget. He answered me that I was very prompt in judging others with my own feelings.... but he said: I suppose that you would not dislike a portion of it even if stolen? I answered in the affirmative, he took the branch and cut me one or two joints! Now, do you realize how I felt when I held a section of that *coveted plant* in my hand? I confess that I forgot for a moment my *disappointment* of that *trinity* of *deceptions* that weighed on my heart when I left Brooklyn. The transgressions of the "*element*" in having passed that resolution on *Foreign exhibitors* the *determination not* to award me any *first* premium, *deserved* or not, and *not expecting* to get my Coleus cuttings, that I got without cutting my fingers! That Coleus was one of the best *weed* that I ever had. A *weed!* Will you say? Well, this qualifying adjective is not my own coining, it belongs to our old friend Mr. Wm. Grey of Albany who described it "a *fine ornamental nettle*" (Urtica urens) a *bad weed* in Europe, any how! I have *felt* its *malignity* on some part of my individual......

long before I studied Cryptogamy. At the time I got it, it proved to be òne of the best "*root of all evils*" this "*root plant*" suggests me more of this same *quality*, but more *weedy* "a *variegated weed*" as would say our *friend above*. It is "Ægopodium podarasia" goutwort, in English, a plant growing as *freely everywhere* as quack or couch-grass (Triticum repens), it is *eminently* a root of *all evils* but it produces both abundance of *roots* and some money, which to my knowledge "*pays better*" than Coleus to-day and gives less trouble, but I think I have said enough if not too much, so I shut the valve....and what next? I hardly know, for I have been led astray, wandering hither and thither without I might say having the conscience of what I was about. I have when on the ground of the Brooklyn Hort. Society forgotten a few incidents, that probably I shall never have occasion to relate unless I do it now. That year 1854, was an eventful remarkable year. First, it was the *advent* or *reviving* — of the Brooklyn Hort. Soc'y, which Society shined for seven years, except a very few cloudy days. It was the *First* year we saw a travelling agent from a European Horticultural establishment on this Continent, at least to my knowledge. It was the year of the *Crimean War* and *not* a Holy *war* but the *reverse*. I say not Holy, perhaps because it somewhat *hurt* my *purse*, a *sensitive* thing with every body. It was the first year I began to import plants (directly) from Messrs. Low of the Clapton Nurseriers, the founder of the establishment, his son, who died lately, was the same man who came hither in 1854 and who came to see me here in Albany, with Mr. Edgard Sander, now a resident of Chicago, this *Mr. Low* who, when he saw me at 15 or 18 yards distant, hallooed me: Are you Mr. Menand? Yes, I answered, when he said again: Mr. Menand! *the fellow* who sold in Brooklyn last May an Ixora coccinea, £4, four pounds, $20. When he spoke these words we shook hands. Well, by God! or something equivalent, you are a lucky fellow or man to sell a plant $20! We would be glad to sell *all our stock Ixora* for that amount. I would like to see those *four pound* plants. We were within 3 or 4 yards of them, they were in hot bed frames behind us. I opened the sashes and showed *them* to him. I had perhaps 6 or 8 dozen of different sizes when he turned round and said: If our plants were as good as these we would not sell the *stock* for 4 *pounds*. I answered him that I believed him, and we continued to talk of something else — of giving him *an order* for some plants, this was the main object of his visit. Then we began to argue about the identity of an *Erica*, he gave it a name different from the one I had. He said my name was *incorrect*. Then I told him you have cheated me for it comes from your establishment. He said it did not. I said again it did. I found after that he was right, but what makes me mention that circumstance it is not the *name*, but the *fact* that that plant was *dead*, and none of us noticed it, and yet Mr. Low was a competent judge in that matter. When he and his friend left me I went with them to Albany, always thinking of my plant (Ericas at that time were my hobby), that it had a green looking appearance but could not realize that it was dead. As soon as I got home I went to see it with a candle — it was night but could not see any indication of its being dead no more than four or five hours before. As soon as day light came I went again, then I did not want spectacles to see it was gone *ad patres* — gone to heaven — *dead*. Since that I have seen many such examples. I once sold one that I knew was *dead*, but the man had selected it among a few of the same kind. That man was a gardener. I sent him that plant with another *alive*. He got them the same day I sent them, and the day following he wrote me I had made a mistake, that he wanted only one. He soon found out he was mistaken not I. Once I sold a Cereus senilis in the same circumstance and the party who got them told me the *dead* one was the best looking of the two. That man was our friend Mr. Wm. Grey!! So this long spun story shows you that gardeners *are* as *infallible* as the Pope that is to say know as much as he does, this I call "*Equality* in face of the *Reason.*

Now that I am stuck in the ruts of prolixity let me continue a little longer about the events that took place in the year *1854.* A few days after Mr. Low was gone as I had promised him I sent him an order *mostly* Ericas and a few other plants; the whole not to exexceed *$70 or $75.* In Sept. or October I received a box containing the plants ordered, at least I think so, but *I guessed!* When I had opened the box I found that the *plants,* the *pots* they were in, *the soil,* the *whole* was like if having been ground by a *mill stone.* So that one could have snuffed the whole like snuff (tobacco) and strange I saved two plants, one Funkia grandiflora that proved to be Funkia alba a plant I had in quantity, and one Genista prostrata, a British plant; one was worth 6 *pence* British, the other one shilling that is all I had for $70 or $75 and six or seven dollars for freight was not that *coining!!* I wrote Messrs. Low and told them the condition of the plant and added if you *feel* as I *do* when spring comes send me again the same lot as you had and charge me only *half* the price agreed; they did and when the plants came I had about for 6 or 8 dollars worth alive. They gave me the particulars of the shipping in Liverpool. All available (steamers) had been chartered by the government to send ammunition, troops and all kinds of supplies to Sebastapol; that they only found a small steamer *overloaded* that would take my box and to have it stowed near the *engine-room* that which accounts for the *snuff* I got and that which also explains you my "*purse hurt*" by the Crimean War. Now, will all this long *rigmarole story or stories* pay you for the candles you will burn for reading them, if you say yes! I will be *satisfied*, but I *have not* done with the transaction, although I did not give it up, for, from that time I began to import from France, Belgium, England; I had awful bad luck, still I persisted. Some plants I imported three *times* before I could get one alive; of Latania rubra, *Phœnicophorium* Scchellarum, Pandamus reflexus, I think I spent $100 before I could get any alive. Pandamus reflexus was the worst but when I had it I did well with it, because I could propagate it, but the Palms I could not, so when I sold them I had to ask a large price what made some of my friends of the *element* say: that I charged awful prices; it may have been so, but if to-day I had nothing to live but what I realized on those plants I could not have *one meal* every day. I could not very well tell how I have made what we have, nothing in particular; but on many I always kept a little of every thing in the line of horticulture, so I could supply almost any thing wanted during the Secession War. It was the *Golden Age* in every way making money,

and emancipating one portion of human kind *! !* ....
when came the "Genesis" of *greenbacks* that some
wiseacres predicted would be good for nothing.
Many believed it. At that time I had to pay a
man $2,000; I did pay with those *green gems*, he
took some in his fingers and waving them he said:
They are not good for that — designing a *fillip* with
his thumb — but I must take them as if they were
gold. At that time a man of Chicago came one day
here in our residence and asked me with a very few
words of introduction: Are you Mr. Menand? I
answered him I was. Well, he said, I am Mr. ——
Thompson, the man who wrote you lately to get a collection of Azaleas. Have you not received my letter?
Yes, sir, I have and here are the plants and the boxes
ready to pack them, but I would not send them without letting you know the *price* of them and a short *description* of the dimensions of the plants. I have written you to that effect. O! he exclaimed, it was of no
use. I knew your plants. I had seen them before at the
Brooklyn Exhibition. It is all right but do not send
them until I come back from New York, whither I am
going to buy some plants for that! and he showed
$*1,000 green-horns*, if you please, for they were all *new-borns*. *Then* I told him in assuming a *becoming attitude* Well, Sir! you are just the man I wanted to see,
and these *1,000* dollars will suit me better than a

pair of kid gloves on my hands. O! but I am not going to give you all that; I wish to keep some for what I may buy in New York. Well before I go to New York I want to see what you have, in order that I should not buy inferior plants. Well, sir, we will show you the whole of our "elephant" that I have *trained* since I was able to understand that *three* are not a *unit* no more than 2 *and* 2 make *three*, but *four* 4. I will show you *all* we have, because when you come back from the Imperial City you will *buy* more, so as to let me have those 1,000 *pictures* to adorn my office or bed room, where I *brew* my horticultural notions and others.... He passed the remark how do you know that I will buy more? I know it, if you speak *earnestly* that you want *so and so*—because you will not find them there better than I have and no cheaper. I do not care about cheaper I want the *best?* *All right*, sir, we agree; it is understood you come again—of course I must, to give you some instructions about shipping, etc. Yes! and buy more plants to absorb the balance of these $1,000 that I am so eager to add to the list of my new plants.... He did come and gave me upward of 900 *dollars* and besides an order for some officinal plants, such as Laurus camphora, Caryophyllus aromaticus, etc., but he never had them. I heard that not long after our transaction he gave up the plants or the green pictures left him—

divorced from him. Is not the quotation "Hodie to me, Cras tibi" true? To-day to me, to-morrow to me.

Some time after that, another citizen of Chicago came to see me on a certain Sunday morning and asked me if I allowed people visiting our establishment on Sabbath Day? I told him I did, and to convince him of my sincerity I told him

> "If you have never done any more harm
> Than to visit a friend, a garden, or a farm,
> On a Sunday, or any other holy day,
> You are sure to go to heaven straightaway."

It was early in the morning I was going to breakfast and offered him to come with me. He said he had had his breakfast at his Hotel in Albany (Delavan House) where he had to stay until 10 or 11 o'clock at night to go to Chicago, and it was for that reason he *broke* the *Sabbath*, and that he wanted to have something to do to *kill* the *time*. On this "deliberate utterance" I made him the observation that he was an *awful* man to *break* the *days* and *kill* the *time*. Well, he said, in talking, in doing so I do not think I do any more harm than many who pray the whole day. I am a sort of an Artist, I do admire nature and if you will as you said, allow me to stay looking round the whole day, I will be much obliged, for I see that you have enough to see to keep me busy until dark. Please go to breakfast. I will walk through your ground and greenhouses and I shall not break any thing nor kill any body. Well, sir, do as you please, I shall not be long. In fact I was not long when one has a temper as mine and he meets such an *Artistic philosopher* he does not miss the opportunity to take lessons of "*wisdom*" that pay better than praying the "Supreme being" to have rain when it is *dry* or *dry* when it *rains* too much. Praying God to change the *laws* of nature!! as well as to say "he *made a mistake*" when he made them!!! ....I say *pray God* with your *heart* and not with your *lips* only. He remained the whole day. I had some visitors who evidently had been *brought* up to the *same school* as the *artist* and your *pseudo-sketcher*. Certain we had what you *call often platonically* a *good time*, but we had it *practically so*, abstraction made, that we had hardly any thing to eat.

On Saturday, the day before, we had got short of bread and we forgot to get some, so on Sunday morning I went in Albany to get some at the Baker or rather the "*Bakress!!*" She would not sell me any, but she began to give me some blessings *in verba canina*. I dare not to tell you in English all the flow of her rhetoric, for I was far off that she was still declaiming, when our horses got afraid of the noise, started, not expecting any oats from such unhospitable inn. Nevertheless we enjoyed. We had some crackers and cheese and wine and "Tom and Jerry" *ad libitum*, for when we had all our crackers eaten we ate or rather we *cracked* jokes.. It was not so indigestible, besides we made up in *fluid* what we were short of in *food*. After dark we broke the meeting and parted. Our artist left me some specimens of his art in the shape of 200 dollars. I have always been sorry since not to have seen him again, and

"If he is dead, I hope he is gone to heaven Artistically
As I hope when I die to go thither horticulturally."

There is pleasure in meeting *genial men* with whom you can exchange your ideas without *bruising* any one's feelings, like our *shrew!* above had done to me *about bread*.

Here a *Retrospective thought* strikes my mind that somewhere in my lucubrations I have spoken of Cryptogamy and Cryptogamic studies, but that I have not given the definitions of my ideas in reference to their *double* meaning. Cryptogamia! indeed! they were (*Hidden*). I have meant to say that by Cryptogamic studies I wanted to study plants deprived of sexual organs, not visible to the naked eye; and also the study of the "*human heart*." Study a thousand times more difficult than to study and analyze the most microscopic, impalpable, embryonic "Mucidinæ" (Meldew family) for there are 75 years I began to try that or those studies, and so far, to-day, I hardly know a few letters of *its alphabet* (of the later, human heart).

As I am narrating retrospective anecdotes, I may as well continue, inasmuch as they all have some relation to horticultural incidents, or to the horticulturist himself.

At one of the Brooklyn horticultural exhibitions I had some Ericas (Heaths). A gentleman of New York, then the king of sugar dealers (I admit kings in commercial affairs and intellectual notions; beyond that *none*), saw them and inquired for me, to know if they were for sale. I was out of the city that day, as I almost always did, when the judges awarded the premiums; not finding me he went for the president of the society, and asked him if those "*Scotch Heaths*" were for sale. He answered him he thought that I might be in want of the amount of their value in money, but that I might also prefer to keep them! Well, he said, I understand that, but tell him that I want them and I will pay what he will ask me. At the close of the exhibition I took them to him; the moment he saw me he took my hand with both of his, and very sympathetically said, you must be a *Scotchman*, to grow such plants — "Scotch Heaths." I told him they were no more Scotch heaths than I was a Scotchman. Well, he said, it does not matter, they suit me and will take the whole of them. How much do you want and what money, gold or bank bills? As you please. He paid me in gold. Then asked me if I had any children? Yes, sir; I have a fair collection of both sexes, and in pairs; four boys and four girls. Do you want to buy some (he had none)? They are not for sale. No, he said; *I have been wishing* some but I did not *want to buy* them. The reason I ask you is, that children are as fond of candies as we are fond of Heaths. So he called one of the young ladies attending the retail store to give me three or four pounds of the best candies. Then he shook my hand, telling me, Mr. Menand, when you get some more of such plants as you have brought me I will take them. I have never sent him any, but the same year or maybe the year after, he and his wife came to Albany to see the State Fair. It was very warm and he could not find anything fit for him to drink on the Fair ground, when he remembered that I was living on the Troy and Albany road, he inquired and he found that I lived close by, so they came. He no sooner saw me that he said, "we are *perishing* for want of a drink; can't you give us some, a Frenchman must have claret; have *you* not got any? Yes, I have; but it is not *Scotch Wine!* He laughed and said, no matter, it will do; so I took them in the house and went for a bottle of Burgundy or Bordeaux wine, I forget, he took the bottle and filled up a quart of his glass and degusted it — " en connoisseur," and told me it is very good, but mine I have home is better! it is older! I felt like telling him, as I heard once a French priest telling a man who had brought hime some fowls from a friend. He, the priest, had given that man a bottle of wine and something to eat, as it is the custom in the country. When he had taken a glass or two of that wine, the priest asked him, how do you like my wine? The fellow seemed to me as if he knew something about wine, or at least he had pretensions. He said, " Monsieur Le Cure," it is very good, but if it was *one year older*, it would be much *better*; it was good wine, but the fellow wanted to show his knowledge of wines, but the priest got so much vexed of that man's impudence that he took the bottle, corked it again, and said to that *churl*, holding the bottle under his nose, you will come next year, it shall *be better* — now! go home. I did not do like the priest, but I told him the story ; he and his wife laughed heartily. That man and his wife were well-bred people, and when he told me his wine was better, because he had paid $30 *per case*, and mine only cost me about fifty cents a bottle. I bought mine by the cask of sixty gallons ; then I asked him if he found his wine $2 a bottle better than mine ; his wife said our's is not *fifty cents* better, the difference was in the *social standing* of that gentleman, he was a millionaire, and I was *wise* for *want* of *money*... He told me, I suppose that wine and you come from the same locality. Yes, sir! and I am trying to improve myself by old age as wine does. It is an old proverb, or aphorism of our ancestors, the "*Gaulois*" that

> "Good old wine and young women
> Give you the illusion of going to Heaven."

Now that I have told you more or less edifying stories—no! *stories* but *histories* (authentic) I may have committed some chronological errors or expressed myself with too much enthusiasm, but all I have said is *truer* than what is often termed "Sacred History."

Just this moment I think of the history of a plant of great intrinsic value, as far as mere money is concerned, but also for the gratification it gives, by its frequency in blooming several times through the whole year, Summer and Winter.

This plant is Vanda tricolor *variety* and tricolor "Corningina" dedicated by his friends to Mr. Erastus Corning, President of "Albany Orchid Club" Orchid Club! I have never heard of such an Association! It may be so, nevertheless it has existed and *gloriously* for many years and some of its members are still alive and ready to vindicate and praise its doings, *collectively,*

not *individually*, it is not here the place to scrutinize the *private* life of any body. We leave that to the "*Judge of the Supreme Court above our heads!*"
.... We probably shall have occasion to make digression on that Club and the Clubbists — so let us return to our Vanda. Here I am somewhat at a loss how to begin the biography of our plant and not *make* too many errors in delineating the character of the incidents connected with it. I will try to do my best; the subject is worthy of attention. As far as I can recollect I imported the plant before the Secession War, for there was no duty on plants at that time. It was imported sometime between 1857 or 1859 about. It was a small plant 3 or 4 leaves for which I had paid $15 or $20. I had it perhaps two years, when Mr. E. Corning (a great lover of plants and flowers, since I knew him (1843) he was a boy then, and I had seen more than one-third of my career) came with two genial friends *evidently*, at first sight, after a *good dinner !* and of course with the usual *irrigations* of liquid in such circumstances. He jumped out of his carriage and came to me with a florid, lively countenance and told me how are you Mr. Menand, and how are the new plants doing? and pointing out a small greenhouse against our dwelling house said: You always keep some good things in that *hole!* It was and is still a small place hardly high enough for a man with a stove

pipe hat. Can I go in? yes you can; he was hardly in when he noticed our *Vanda*, though he did not know then a Vanda from a Dendrobium. Is not that an Orchid? I told him it was. Have we got it? I do not know; you ought to. No! but you know better than I do what we have, for we get almost every thing from you; how much is it worth? I did not believe he wanted to buy any thing any more than I wanted to drown myself, so I told him I suppose that to-day you could buy one in London for about what I paid, $15 or 20. Well, he said I will take it; very well! but I do not want to sell it. I have only this one; I keep it. By J.... or some other expression, I ask you how much it is worth; I give you the maximum price, $20, and you say you do not want to let me have it. It is mine; so saying he put his hand in his vest pocket to pay me, but he had no money. When I saw him in that mood I thought it was no use arguing, and I told him you will pay me with a few other items you owe me. No! I want to pay it right away, so he called one of his two friends and said J. B. C. lend me $20. What! he answered, you must have a good reputation for solvability if you cannot be trusted for such an amount. He will trust me, but I see that if I do not pay him he will not send me the plant; he was right; when I found he had no money I made up my mind at once that I would not send the plant, thinking after he would be gone he would forget it, but he insisted to pay; he read in my face as I read in his mind, but he had the advantage over me, so he asked his friend again for $20; the friend told him from outside, for he was out and we were inside: Erastus! you know me well enough; I never lend money to any body without knowing what use he is going to do with the money. By .... I have told you already to pay for that plant. What plant — I want to see it; he walked in, looked at the plant for one second and went out backward, so that he knocked his head against the top of the door, turned round, picked up his hat, took his cigar out of his mouth and assuming a theatrical attitude, as an actor acting the part of Hamlet when going to recite the monologue: To be or not to be! and said by .... !! 25 dollars for a plant !! do you know that with $25 we could, the three of us, get completely.... intoxicated with Lord *Byron's Intoxication* (in a measure). As Lord Byron's *intoxication* is, "par excellence," the triplicate effusion of the heart, of the soul, and of the most sensitive part of the human intellect! A Trinity of thing celestial, an union of bliss! " E pluribus unum——*spiritual*!!"

After that *tirade* I was going to tell him, you are right enough and you cannot improve your condition; but I kept my tongue and I began to reconsider my visitors. The *senior* of the trio had been, during all the time of our transaction, walking to and from, but always keeping at a distance from us. He was a very *eminent* man, by his *individuality*, being connected with the Hudson River R. R. and N. Y. Central R. Road, and besides a member of congress; so he had to take care of himself, and he did. It was plain to me that his two young copartners *tried* to get him out of his *centre* of *gravity!* but so far had failed; for I have never known how they reached Albany, but I had good reasons to think when they got in the city our disciple of Aristotle did not continue his exercise of peripatetic in walking in the streets of Albany, as the followers of Aristotle did, in the Lyceum of Athens. I learned the day after that Mr. Corning had been to his farm at Kenwood to see Mr. Grey, his gardener, and let him know that he had *stuck* the Frenchman in buying a plant that he would not sell, etc. When our friend Grey came, after he had shaken my hand, he asked me if it was true, that I had sold my *unique* Vanda to Mr. Corning, for $20 or $25; for I am not sure. I have said somewhere that I could never learn arithmetic, and it would be no wonder if I have confounded three or four for four and five. Grey told me, you must have been out of your mind or *drunk* when you made such a silly bargain, for a few months before I had offered you $40 for it, and as much for an Ærides crispa majus, and you would not sell them to me. Now, said Grey, so that you cannot repair the blunder you have done, send us that Ærides for $40, and $20 you have had for the Vanda, will make your loss lighter. Mr. Corning has told me, as soon as that plant produces an offset we will give it to you. And, mind; nobody at that time knew what it would be until it bloom. Now, if I was asked how long it was before it bloom, I could not tell to save my life. From the time the plant left me until *1880*, all is confusion in my mind. All I know is what our friend Grey has told me, that they gave me a plant; but when, I can't tell. But it must be, because in *1873* I sold a plant to Mr. *E. S. Rand*, who is now at Para, Brazil, but who lived in Boston then ; and I sold that plant *without knowing it was* Vanda *Corningiana !!* You sold a plant without *knowing what* it was? Yes! Well, it is carrying the jokes a little too far. It seems so ; I *admit it*. It will be a little lengthy to explain, but I cannot avoid explanation, or else everybody would call me an *idiot*, if nothing else. In *1873* Mr. Rand bought a Vanda *suaris*. He picked, selected it *himself*, among a few plants. I had the plant in the shed to be packed, with all the other ones he had selected, orchids and other plants, when my wife came and looked at them, *especially* to the *Vanda* he had selected, and told me, you are not going to send that to Mr. Rand? It is a *mean* looking plant. It was not *bad*, but when compared with the other Vandas I had, it did not look well. Why do you not give him one of those good looking? I would. I have offered him one, but he would not have it; they are V. tri-color, and he wants V. *suaris Veitchii, which were* and *are* all *tri-color!!* in varieties with different adjectives, as Messrs. Veitch have demonstrated in their *admirable!!* Manual of Orchidaeous Plants. My wife said so much about that *mean* plant to be changed for one of the other good looking, that I did it, but I felt I was doing *wrong*, although it was my conviction then, as to-day, that all these *Vandas* were all *tri-color*, strictly, *botanically* speaking. Four years later we found that plant to be V. tri-color *Corningiana*, and not thought much more than the other varieties. We had not had time to appreciate it, at least *I*, who ought to have known as much as anybody else, except *Grey*, and as I have said, I have not begun to appreciate it before *1880*, as far as I can recollect. When I had a splendid plant, perhaps two and one-half or three feet high, with *three* shoots starting at the base of that plant, the *only one I had;* it was in bloom; when one of our neighbors, a *newly sprung orchidophile*, who had caught the orchid fever to exacerbation, to the paroxism! asked me if I would sell it to him. I said that I would not sell it until I had separated the young ones; he asked me again how long it would be; I told him I could not say exactly, but as soon as they would break root he could have the plant for $100. It was agreed, but he was so impatient to get it that two or three times a week he was after me to know when I would send it to him. A few days later he came again, when I just cut two of the three; then he said, I hope you will send it to me to-day. No! there is one more to cut; in a few days you will have it. He went grumbling that I wanted the money and keep the plant. I did not hear him, but my phanerogyne (wife) heard him, and when he was gone she told me, you have better send it to him; he is like a child. I know he is like a child, yet, I can not to keep him from crying give that offset which is worth at least $25, and more. Well, she said, he is a good fellow, a good customer, he always pays you what you ask him; you can afford to let him have it as it is, and she used a rather — *homely* expression, but at the same time very expressive — *incisive*. She said, you — " you may give him the young *calf*, you have charged him enough for the *cow*." You will soon see that I had not charged too much for the *cow*, and to give the *calf* into the bargain; in less than two or three weeks he sold the CALF for $50 to a Florist in Albany, who, two weeks later sold it to *Mrs. Morgan* of New York, for $100. One year later the man who had bought my *cow plant*, sold it by auction in New York for $225, to the same man

who had bought the *calf*, and he sold it again to the
same lady, Mrs. Morgan, for $300. In less than one
year, or two, I don't know exactly, I sold the *two calves
first weaned*, to a *Drover*.... of Orchids in Troy, for
$225, and at that price because he was my friend, and
he is so yet, in 1892.... I have an idea that some will
whisper in each other's ear; that "*Albany Dutchman*
must be an *awful boaster* with his *rigmaroles!* I accept
the expressions, *Albany Dutchman* and *rigmaroles*, but
not boaster. I am not a boaster, unless you understand
by boaster, a man who tells the *truth without meta-
phor—circumlocution*, then I am a *boaster*, and proud
of it.

"Now you may possibly ask yourself if that overstretched history of a plant will close the dams of my
overflowing vein? I would do it *at once* if I thought
you were tired of trampling in thickset of obscure, and
often unmeaning digressions.... but my vanity
prompts me to go on, for I have not yet exhausted my
stock. After this, another.

Don't you say in English, " the more the merrier?"
Well then, you can not complain if I understand a little of the *genius* of your mother tongue, and try to
apply it, that is my way of learning *abstruse* philosophy, and the English into the bargain. Some day
when I have leisure, and if I do not *slip* off from that

slippery, steep *slope* we call *life*, I will ask you some questions of English language that I have not been able to learn to my satisfaction, in *half a century*. For the present I will make some reflexions on what I can say that will relieve your *"Ennui"* to hear always the same song. What could I say that would keep you awake?

I think I have spoken of our Orchid Club and its members, how would you like a diagnostic of the clubbists? If they were not the best of men, they were not either the worst, they were so, so, *collectively* as I have hinted before, they were all *gentlemen*, although of different types, as regards tastes, of moral and material things, and as I have told you and tell you again. *We* — I ought to say to be *polite*. They were *all good men, and I* was trying to be so also. I must tell you between ourselves. They *all* had the *tools* to behave gentlemanly, though the tools do not always do good work, they often "kind o' fails if used improperly, in the wrong way, you may try any way, but mus' n't take the wrong one, " sez he," or else.... They had different tastes in the line of Orchids, for instance: Our President, Mr. Corning, said he liked better Odontoglossum *Crispum*, etc. Mr. Dinsmore, not having the same optical faculties, preferred *Cattleya*; another inclined to *Vanda cœrulea*, Vanda Corningiana, Angraenm citratum, etc. Another said he liked

Orchids, but would rather have *Champagne!!* Another liked *The Spectabile* (he meant: Cypripedium spectabile), with Mrs. Menand's Punch, flavored with cherry *bounce* (cherries preserved in brandy). Another said he would like to see pretty Orchids, *sweet scented*, very *fragrant*, fasten on the bosom of a pretty young woman, and been allowed to smell them on that spot, so you see how tastes differed. I suppose you would like to know what I preferred? primo: I preferred my "phanerogyne" secundo: I like BOTH, the whole Cypripedium family, and all the other genera spoken of above Odontoglossum .... *Cattleya*, etc., etc.... I forgot I like also good Sauterne Wine, and I do not dislike Champagne nor any *good company*, this to my mind is *preferable* to all the others, but both *good* company and good refreshment will complete the festival, and make a man happy if he is a *man who* can control his will. And here I must say that during several years we kept together, I never saw one out of the way of decency but *once*. We were *almost all present* at the meeting. We had to welcome a lot of New Orchids and other plants arrived from England. Among them was a variegate species of Agave that will deserve a special notice that I probably shall do if I live long enough. On that remarkable day in the history of our Club we *irrigated* so — much our *notions* that when night came and we had to return to

Albany in two or three carriages waiting for us *I noticed* that we were all, I thought — what you call in English "half seas over;" No! not quite so, but what the French call to be "Dans les Vignes du Seigneur" literally in English "In the vineyards of the Lord." When we left Mr. Corning's place and before we got in the carriages I *cast a look* at the *whole* company and I concluded that not one of our company of Trojans of whom I was one of them, were in a condition to think to give a gratification to the drivers who had been waiting for us perhaps an hour or more so. I did it although I thought I was not much better than all the rest, but you will see when *men* are *men* and determined to be so what they will do. When we arrived to Albany we found we had missed the train we wanted to go by, so we had to wait one hour. You probably suppose that during that one hour we would to kill the time, to *irrigate ourselves* again. Well, we did it, we went in a restaurant where I had never been, where we drank every one of us a cup of tea, nothing else. Was not that heroic!!! This happened 10 or 12 (or more) years ago. From that time our meetings became less frequent and our enthusiasm followed the same progression i. e., went backward. Our last proselyte, neophyte, had to give up his collections; that which *cooled* our energy; for he was a *powerful stimulant*, two strong for his constitution — for his own good, and it somewhat re-acted on us. Yet, after that the Orchid fever did not abate at once. Another amateur (not of our locality) stepped on his track for a few years then collapsed as any undertaking conducted too recklessly will come to sooner or later.

This digression reminds me that I have not concluded my description of the different *tastes* of our *conclubbists* for different kinds of Orchids. I have not given entirely the enumeration of what I liked or did not. After having said that I liked *good company above* all I ought to have said that I was a sort of *pantophile* ("lover of every thing,") with *many exceptions* such as ill-treatment, hypocrisy, counterfeit money, foul language, the smell of rank tobacco, the polemics of politicians who are to-day *protectionist* when they have goods for sale at home inferior to foreign goods, or *free traders*, when they have to import what they have not or cannot produce. I suppose you have a *"quantum sufficit" of what I like and do not. Now you know a little about our peculiarities. To complete your knowledge, I must (notwithstanding my *modesty*) tell you that I was somebody in that association of good fellows. I was a sort of a sub-honorary *janitor*, a *connecting* link between the dissident parties when there were

---

(* Quantum sufficit — plenty enough, too much.)

any; and there had been *one* in which I acted a very important part in, I reconciliating two of the *best men* (every one in his way) I have ever seen or known and I have done it *unknown* to them, until done but not how; the matter between them was of a very *delicate* nature and the parties more *sensitive* yet. I had to use a great deal of *diplomacy* or maybe of *vice!* according to my notions (etymological) for I did not think I could practice *diplomacy*, which expression conveys to my mind the *fanciful idea* of " *double maker* " of *mischief* as it has done often in *international affairs* causing *bloody wars* between two friendly nations and all that caused by *diplomatists set at work* by *miserable wretches* not worth the ROPE or the AXE they ought to have been dispatched to hell with such as that *ne plus ultra debased scoundrel*, Napoleon the *Third*, that *arrant, nefarious beastly* human being, sustained by such *worthies* as " *Bazaine* " and " tutti quanti" of the same *breed*. Excuse me this onslaught on venomous wild or rather *civilized wild* beasts. I could not refrain making this explosion of my bile — choler ....

Let us return to our litigation of *our friends* again! and more intimate than ever before, until one of them *departed*, the one *who stuck* his preference on the " *Spectabile* " and Madame Phanerogyne's punch flavored with cherry bounce — the one ever ready to plan an excursion to the haunts of Spectabile— the main spring of our complicated mirth machinery and always with the countenance of *a* judge presiding a *criminal court* or as Mr. Corning defined him: As an *undertaker* who would have lost his wife.... If? he had *loved her* when she lived. That *genial* man whose *seriousness* was so rigid in appearance, could be dissolved with the simple chemical preparation of two or three *good jokes* and one or two glasses of good Sauterne wine, or in presenting him with a bouquet of *spectabile*, or any other flowers, and in presenting him the flowers or a French " *Bouillon* " and a glass of cherry wine, and tell him, " This for *fraternity's* sake ! " This word, that I think I used for the first with him, would literally galvanize him. Let him " Requiescat in pace." *All thy friends will remember thee as long as they live*, especially thy "connecting link"—L. M. Here I only speak for myself, and very likely the other *links* of our *chain* feel the same. So, Adieu! adieu !! *perhaps? resurgamus* in Cypripedibus ! We shall " Resuscitate in Cypripediums!!"....

Shall I continue to give the diagnosis of our members? Mr. Corning, our president, was in some respects a fit match for our departed friend, the " *spectabile*," to whom Mr. Dinsmore, of Staatsburgh-on-the-Hudson, could be added to complete a triumvirate of consummate experts in theoretical jokes, and occasionally *practical* ones. These three together, could have entertained our company a whole night. Alas! of those three genial men two are gone forever, and at this very moment one of our most eminent members, our old friend Mr. Wm. Grey, Mr. Corning's gardener, is very dangerously sick.... To close these sketches of our friends, and for the "Bonne Bouche," delicious morsel, I will introduce you to my — our friend, Mr. A. R. Smith, the *Trojan drover* of *calves- Vanda Corningiana*, the brothers and sons of the *cow and calf* that were sold to Mrs. Morgan, of New York, the: *personified Providence* of the *Orchids dealers* of both continents, American and European.

Our last *link*, for being the *Omega, the last*, is not the less important for his collection of orchids, but is next to Mr. Corning, and at one time Mr. Corning sighed for the possession of some orchids he had, especially for a specimen of "Phalænopsis *grandiflora aurea*," as we have never seen its equal since, and even to-day he has specimens of Cymbidium eburneum, Cymbidium Mastersianum, Cymbidium Lowianum, Lowianum, from three to six feet in diameter, Coelogyne cristata, Coelogyne Ocellata maxima and Coelogyne, Massangena, etc., inferior to none. Of Mr. Corning's collection of all kinds of orchidiacæ. It is useless to enumerate, they are too well known. Just now he has Cypripedium, *Spiccrianum, cardinale, Schroderianum*. For one of them I would give my *head if* I could see, *the plants*, after it would be off my shoulders. *I hope!* you will understand that this last phrase of mine is *platonical!*.... old as my head is I would not give it for an orchid, and besides, if I was willing to make such a bargain, nobody would accept it; one would rather have a large pumpkin, or.... anything else.

I have mentioned somewhere that our club had its meetings once in a while, here and there; that is, with *one* exception, at Mr. Corning's suburban villa, or here at our "rus in urbe," bicoque, or shanty, in English. I say bicoque or shanty, paltry house, because I have heard that Cæsar (that heroic butcher), had said to his satellites and company, that he preferred to be the *first* in a *shanty* than the "*second*" in Rome. So do I; I prefer to be living in a shanty *paid for*, than in a palace mortgaged for more than its value; or drink a cup of tea or coffee, than the best champagne drunk before *paid*, and *often* never paid at all. I don't remember if when our meetings met here at our *nest* — what nest? will you say, the *nest* where I kept my *rara avis*, that *flew* from *Astoria* to *Albany* — do you forget? I do not know if our members found the reception we gave them equalled to Mr. Corning's; but I am sure we did the best we could in our sphere of action, and I recollect well that at one time we had a certain wine named *Barsac*, that *loosened* the tongues *amazingly*, in spite of you.

I forget that some years before that *Barsac episode*, we, my friend, Mr. A. R. Smith and I, had bought a cask of white wine, German or French, I forget, that was so exhilarating when you had *drunk* a small glass full, you felt like flying! Any how, it made one talk more than he ought to, telling you what he had done, and what he would in the future. The color of that wine was so seducing, so bewitching, so sympathetic, that when you had enough you wanted more! like " Oliver Twist!!" only the former had too much and the latter not enough.

That wine was so tempting I cannot find English expression to describe its influence on one's system, all I can recollect to-day is that Mr. Smith and I decided in our *wisdom* it was the best preparation you could administer to a man on whom you wished to make some psychological observation. Finely we baptized it " Rayons du Soleil!! Rays of the Sun!! We never had since so good. The next we had after was so inferior that we called it the " Rays of the Moon," and it hardly deserved that name. Since I am born I have never seen such wine. When you had a small glass on your stomach it immediately went to your head, just like a pan of milk on the fire, ran over and set instantly the moment you take it off. The sensation you felt in your head was *celestial!* .... but of short duration but!..

From this lengthy dissertation I expect that those who may read it will think that I am a *worshipper* of wine, naturally. Speaking so enthusiastically of wine and drinking it. I am no more a *devotee* to liquors than you are of drinking cold water to excess. This sort of apology made let us speak no more of it. But of what shall I speak of ? Not of the Orchid Club, although I have another *sitting* to recount, but not immediately. We have had enough of Orchids, *too* much, for since many years I have often, in a measure, *cursed* them, for they have been the principal cause of the *neglect* in which all other kinds of plants have fallen, and there are many more interesting that good many Orchids hardly worth the water they drink!! I pray you! *infeverished* orchidists or orchidophiles or *both*, do not take it too hard if I *jeer* your hobbies! Our *orchidomania*, it has *hurt* my *pantomania* if I am permitted to use such an expression, *seemingly* " far-fetched and dear bought!" With reason I say *dear bought;* for many of the plants I have bought of late years *are now* commercially speaking *worthless!* and I charge your *monomania* to have worked that *plague* that *ostracism* against any thing which is not *Orchids* or *Roses*.

I shall have sometning more to say about Orchids, etc., etc. I am trying to remember if I have not forgotten some incidents connected with my intimate life, and I find that I have overlooked perhaps the most important event of my life, except my *binding* with the chains of matrimony. It is the celebration of the anniversary of my seventieth birthday in *1877*, epoch of the most flourishing of *our Club* and also of our business, and every thing else connected with private horticulture. We were all under the impression of that first *grand* international exhibition in Philadelphia, *1876*. At that time our lover of *Spectabile*, and also our *proselyte* who bought the *Vanda !* were both alive. These two, with probably some others unknown to me, had a consultation with my wife about their mutual desire to have me celebrating my birthday without letting me know what they intended to do, and asked her if she was a woman who could *keep a secret*. She answered them she thought she could, but wanted to know what it was before BINDING herself. They did, and she kept the secret so well that I did'nt know any thing but the day of the ceremony. The preparations could not be kept secret for me, but the details *nothing*. Only one

day or two before the 2d *of August* my wife asked me if
I would pay a bill of $30 or about she was about to make.
I said I would but I ought to know. She said she could
nor would not tell me. You will know after. I want
"carte blanche" for every thing, and she had her own
way, and I have never had such a day since. We had one
of our greenhouses empty that one of *our* friends dec-
orated with palms, etc., where a table had been fixed
for fifteen or more persons; and next to that house
another separated from where we sat, that we could
not see inside of it. My wife had a band of music
that none of us *clubbists* and *others* knew nothing about.
It was only at desert, when we began to drink champagne that we heard the band of music playing the
Marseillaise, Yankee Doodle, etc. And at that time, *moment, minute,* our friend the *Spectabile!* placed in my
plate a little box, containing a splendid gold watch, with
the names engraved of same of the members of our
club. I was so much surprised that for a few seconds
I was *speechless.* I could not say yes! and yet, as a
rule, I talk *too much.* The hearing of that music and
the presentation of that watch galvanized me for many
seconds, for I did not expect any such things for a surprise; it was a *surprise!!* that made me feel *proud*
of being *seventy years old,* although it is the age of the
decline of life, when a man is considered no longer a
man *in the real* acceptation of the word *man!* But

after I had recovered from the *commotion*, and being able to analyze my feelings and retrospective thoughts, I felt half *intoxicated* with delight, and considering that all those friends were men with *religious creed* and principles diametrically opposed to mine in many respects, and with some in politics also ; and yet.... any one can draw his conclusions ; as for me, *I felt*, and to this day *I feel*, in the *deepest* recess of my *soul*, of my *heart*, a sensation of *more* than *delight*, but that I cannot define to my satisfaction. I can feel, but I can't describe, *how*, I have received so much respect and devotion from men so different of me, in many respects. All that I can tell is that I feel something like of an *immense vanity* for attentions paid to me in many circumstances in the course of my life, and that, *several times* from people who had *calumniated* me *in a scandalous* manner, and who after rendered me justice *so spontaneously* as they had defamed me. *One instance*, in which I take pleasure in relating. When I was corresponding with the *being!* who became my consort for fifty years, she lived with some *lukewarm* friends in Albany who did not like my correspondence with the above person, because it thwarted their views in some ways. The *lady friend* told her that she ought not to correspond with such a *man, that* they knew (they had been told) that I was an *awful bloody* Republican, who would kill a man like a fly;

that besides being a Republican ! that I had *a wife* and several *children* in *France*....and the rest of the eulogy ran in the same direction. Was not such a recommendation fit to help me in *winning* the *heart* of that woman? However, she listened to the advice but continued to correspond with me, without giving me information of the "*platonic wife and children ;*" but she wrote me about some things she wanted to know. I answered the letter immediately, with the alacrity of a *lover bona fide !* but at the same time a little wounded in his dignity. I wrote a letter of four pages of large paper, where I gave a rapid *sketch* of my life (not as this one I am writing to-day, but one that would carry conviction in any soul who would have had a doubt). I have that letter yet, and many others from both of us. As she had received that letter and just done reading it, the *lady friend ! ?* came, while she had the letter in her hands. She said, Miss Jackson! notwithstanding what we have told you, you continue to correspond with that *man ! ? ! ?* The Miss Jackson, the *timid bird*, but with a strong mind, answered her, yes, madam! I have ; and I was going to show you the letter, to read it with care ; then to give me your impression, after reading it ; and according to your answer I shall *break* the correspondence or *continue* it. *Please read on.* It must have taken her at least half an hour to read it, because it had been written in wonderful agitation, excitement, wrath, indignation, despised love — I thought, but I soon found I was mistaken. That letter was a specimen of Egyptian (hieroglyphs). Written in French! as we corresponded. When she had read it she stood in front of that Miss Jackson and said :

Mon enfant ! l'homme qui a écrit une lettre comme celle-ci n'est pas un homme *ordinaire !* et vous n'avez pas voulu le croire, cette homme là sent *vivement* et vous avez douté de sa veracité, vous avez en tort ! . . . .

ENGLISH OF THE ABOVE: My child ! the man who has written such a letter is not an *ordinary* man ; he feels *vividly,* he expresses his emotions with *warmth*; and you have doubted his veracity ; you have been wrong !

You understand this *spontaneous* confession ? Compare it with the *bloody Republican!* etc., and draw your conclusion. . . .

Now, I'll tell you; I *felt ten times* more *gratified* of that *candid confession* than I had been *vexed,* indignant, of the *calumny.* In plain English, my *vanity* was high flattered. Some other time I shall tell you another historical anecdote almost *similar,* with a very eminent man in *his* sphere, at the time, in Jersey City. But it was not a *love quarrel,* but a horticultural *nonsense,* as we are all *liable* to do.

Since that anniversary of mine in 1877, our "*Spectabile*," Mr. Pierson of Troy, managed to induce us to have another, in 1879, under the pretext that we ought to have an *opening!* on account of having built a new greenhouse, and by doing so we should kill two birds with one stone. We did it, and our club association presented me again with a token of their friendship, in presenting me, not a watch, but something as valuable, if not more; a sort of "pabulum animi;" "food for the mind," the American, Appleton's Encyclopedia. Two or three years later they presented me for the third time, with a handsome set of crystal glasses, in all varieties, for all kinds of wine and other liquors. I, *of course*, expressed my gratitude, but, I made the observation that they had made a mistake; they ought to have presented me with as many varieties of wine and liquors as they had given me of different shape glasses; that we could drink good wine in ordinary glasses, if we had anything to drink; but we could not drink without some liquid. Well! he said, always our promoter, the "*Spectabile*," we might have done so, but we did not want to *trust* our *tastes* in such a delicate matter as a choice of *beverage*. We thought it would be better to leave that to you, a man who had spent thirty years of his life in the two best provinces of France, producing wines, such as "Burgundy and Champagne." We know the value of crystal ware but not of wine. So you see that we have acted wisely, is it not? Besides, when wine is drunk there is nothing left but empty bottles, useless; but the glasses may be used "*ad libitum;*" "when you have something to put in." Anyhow, these glasses might be used for the future generations of orchids' clubs, who could drink your health when you will be gone to Heaven, where we sincerely hope you will go when you will leave us, unless you should prefer to go whither you may meet your *nightmare* Mr. *Linden* who swindled you "on that" *line* bifurcated line you said,. in 1877.

Here ends nearly our Orchid club frolics — sub-scientific evolutions. Some of us had tried to keep up the "*Sacred fire,*" but our *combustible* was exhausted, and our last neophyte, proselyte who had the "*stimulant*" had given up his office where he kept the *holy matches* to light the *sacred fire*, which *burned his* fingers, then later our "*Spectabile*" had also departed (suddenly); then another member, Capt. of a steamboat on I — was going to say the "Styx!" that river "*Lethe*" makes me forget every thing! I meant the *Hudson river*, so we hardly had a quorum left. So that since we have been living on our former reputation. Yet we have a few remainders of our laurels. "Sic transit gloria Mundi." "Thus fades the glory of the world."

Here I beg permission to introduce a parenthesis on a foreign subject to the one above, but which is a reminiscence of my individuality.

A few persons of my acquaintance have made me the remark that they like enough my digressions on any subject I write upon, but am too imaginative, my allusion and quotations are too cloudy, obscure, in short to speak as I do too cryptogamic (hidden.) Maybe it it is so, but I cannot very well refrain myself from doing it. It is inherent to my way of expressing my ideas. When I write I do so exactly as I feel, as I think, just to suit my vague notions, always going ahead and anxious to get at the end of what I have to say, that often I leap over many words, and probably you have noticed it. I know it but I cannot help it, yet I try hard. Next another peculiarity I have, when talking of men, I always or almost take it for granted that all men are *men*, more or less endowed with a certain amount of intelligence. It seems to me that to think differently would be a disguised insult. In my opinion the best way to make a man is to let him understand *he is so !* And if he sees and is convinced he is deficient, he will likely try to get what he is deprived of; if not you have lost your time .... but you have not offended his pride. I know there are men generally styled *smart !* (I use the word as I have heard people using it, but it does not exactly *touch* the *chord* of my understanding in many ways) who would make a dollar where others could not make the fraction of one cent, but in intellectual affairs are quite *green* although with *white hair*. I just remember a very *pleasant instance* to illustrate what I have said above.

Once I had a correspondent in New York to whom I wrote that since I had seen him, I had seen two of his friends. *Both are now dead;* both were or had the reputation of being *smart*, but one was *smarter;* he had much more money than the other, and of course was superior and perhaps he was really so ! Both came to pay me a *friendly ? ?* visit ; for what I did not know. They were *both antipathetic* to me as I was to them, in a measure. I had absolutely nothing to interest them for one was almost *physically blind* and the other *only morally* so, but both had what you call a "*fellow-feeling*," both were well matched. I felt like to ask them what the devil has induced you to come and see me ? But according to what I have told you *supra* I did not; on the contrary, as it was a warm day, I offered them refreshment. They did not accept. So far all right. They thanked me and I went away. It was the same day I wrote to my correspondent the word "*sub rosa*" not to mention the above "*panegyric* of his friend above." He could *not* very well read my handwriting, so he went to see a friend of him who could decipher my hieroglyphics, *Mr. Y. Murkland*, who explained him the contents of my letter, but he was not satisfied; he maintained that I wanted roses, but did not say how many I wanted nor the kind. Mr. Murkland told him I wanted none *at all*. By God! he said: look at the *word Rosa;* does it not mean Roses? No! it means for you *not* to tell your friend what he has written to you, but he *add* that you can do it if you feel so; he *does not care*.

Now you will perhaps believe that I think that man was an ass, *not a bit of it;* he was as *smart* as any one called so; he was ignorant of the meaning of that word, but he had no pretensions. *Ignorance* is not *stupidity* but if he had any pretension to know things that *he did* not he would be *stupid*, that's my way to define ignorance. I do not not know *Hebrew*, yet I do not consider myself an idiot because I am not a polyglot. See what it is to have too much modesty. I say that I do not know Hebrew language when I do! *Amen!* is Hebrew and *I know it* in English and French, etc. So I am a polyglot also!

Now I have better to return to my subject, digressions on *smartness*—as a rule the community judge by the *label* in the *scale* where the merits of men and things are appreciated according to their *specific weight* (in money) not in sterling value. The why! they came to see me has always *puzzled* my mind. It was not *love* for certain. I am at a loss unless they wished to see if I was always the same animal of old time. For many years and perhaps to-day yet, I have been a sort of *curious beast, not mischievous,* and not willing to bark with all sorts of hounds .... for them I was always the " Albany *Dutchman.*" It is not everybody who can be a *Dutchman* and being born in *France!* and besides claiming to be a *Yankee!* in the *good sense* of the word; I feel proud to be a *Yankee,* at least Yankeefied *morally*, if not physically. I am proud to be ever so Yankeefied when I hear our Uncle *Sam* say:

>God means to make this land, John ! ! !
>   Clear thru, from sea to sea ! !
>Believe an' understand, John,
>   The *wuth* o' bein' free ! ! !
>   Ole Uncle S. Sez he, "I guess,
>   God's price is high," sez he ;
>   " But nothin' else than wut He sells
>   Wears long, an' thet J. B.
>   May learn like you an' me ! ! ! "

Amen !
>   " Vive la Republique ! ! !
>   The Sun God and liberty ! ! !
>   And down with politic iniquity."

Here in this moment I drop my pen and rub my forehead to rest, to meditate on what we have done since I came to *light.* I could not see the light, but the light saw me, and I think has since lighted me through my accidental life, which I suppose is now near to its end, and yet I do not think I have stored much wisdom in that lapse of time—*84 years*—I cast a retrospective look on the time past; I consider in bulk, *en masse*, all that we have done, and seen since nearly a century and I cannot realize all the wonderful, marvellous events that have been accomplished in the human life. It bewilders my understanding. The discovery and application of electricity, steam navigation, railroad, the velocity with which we live and *also die!* I wanted to rest, and I perceive that I am philosopHASTRING (for philosophizing) like if I had the conviction to moralize the whole world. I come to think I have better to continue my digressions on useless matters that give me an occasion to *prate*, to *exercise* my pragmatical notions .... after all I think it is my privilege, the privilege of old folks, to be *loquacious*, besides with *me*, it is a *hygienic necessity* to let off the superabundance of foolish ideas which condense in *what* takes the place of my *brain*. So pray! be indulgent for old men ; you may also get *old* and wishing to babble as I do. I will rest a little, then perhaps I shall recollect some anecdotes to relate. Amen! for the time being.

Now that I have rested a little I can resume the current of my *spinning* phrases that I am afraid will wear out the patience of those who may try to read them. I have given the diagnosis of several of the members of our Orchid Club, but I have forgotten one — of Mr. Dinsmore of Staatsburgh on the Hudson, a great lover of all kinds of vegetation, trees, shrubs, orchids, roses, foliage, plants, and above all *jokes* in which he was a specialist. One day he came with two friends; one was a Mr. —— Wells, of Buffalo. I believe the other one a Trojan, not of the ancient city of Asia Minor, but Troy, N. Y., named Virgil, not Virgil the Latin poet, but an expressman living in Troy. Mr. Dinsmore with his *cheerful* and *dignified* manner told *me*, Mr. Menand I have the pleasure to introduce these two gentlemen friends of mine, one is Mr. —— Wells belonging to an express association of Buffalo, who does not care much for plants except the *fermented juice* of the *grape vine* or the *distilled* seeds of rye or wheat. The other one is Mr. Virgil to whom you can tell all your *jaw-breaking names* of plants; he understands *Latin* as the author of the *Bucolics*, etc., then burst into an inextinguishable laughing, in which the *four* of *us participated*, Mr. Dinsmore and I particularly. I did not know if Mr. Wells understood the joke, but Mr. Virgil's laugh was *bitter sweet*, for I do not think he knew what was *Virgil* the poet. I thought from his look that he had an idea he was the laughing stock, but I was not sure. However, Mr. Dinsmore and I enjoyed. As we are at it I may as well finish my *evening* in introducing you to Mr. Dinsmore, and let you know his *humour*. As we were walking through our green houses looking at plants, he said: Menand! you have very fine plants but by God! *he said* you charge for them like the devil — you *skin* — you *rob* people! ain't it? Maybe I do, "but one thing is certain, if you had never robbed your customers any more than I have robbed mine," to-day you could not afford to buy any! Why? because you would have no money to pay for! He laughed and said: An expressman is not a gardener! I know it, a gardener can only rob his customers in *retail* and only once in a long while; whilst the express man robs the public *Daily — Wholesale* and *retail all the year round*. You probably think he got mad? Not the least, for in less than half an hour I had sold him for $200 or more, and every time he came he acted about the same; he lived upon jokes as bees on honey. Many persons have told me he was a *rough, coarse* man; perhaps he was *in words* but not in actions as far as I have known, and I have dealt with *him* 25 or 30 years and I have *known* some of his *deeds* in *philanthropy* that many *sanctified hypocrites* would not have done unless every body had *seen them* doing good, when he would do good *in secret!!!* I have known a *philanthropic* lady, Mrs. Miller, in his immediate locality, *Rhinebeck*, Dutchess county, N. Y. who told me she did not like him; that he was what I have said above. I tried to talk with her to change her convictions, but she would not hear, and yet she was a *benevolent woman, exceedingly so!* but she had preventions against him, she was prejudiced. It is only many years later that I got the knowledge of *Mr. Dinsmore's occult charity* — without ostentation. That lady was dead or I would have told her what he had done with his "*rough bark.*" When talking of good actions I must mention this lady I am talking about. It was during the Secession War. I had sold her a lot of plants, and I had promised her to go and set them in the greenhouse. When done she said, do you not think it would require a few more to look good, they are too far apart. I *agreed with her* — of course. Any one, a gardener or an expressman do not object to receive money. Well, she replied, I can afford it; I have so much money to spend for my pleasure; now, I ask your advice; which is the best to spend the money I have in buying *more plants* or dispose of that money for the *poor wounded soldiers* and other *needy people?* That argument was *ad hominem.** I answered, Madam, I would be glad to get that money for plants I have to sell, but your *appeal* to my judgment is *such* that I

---

* Argument that goes to heart, conscience of a man.

say : Dispose of that money for what you propose, for the *soldiers* and other human beings, suffering, from that *fratricide* war; be benevolent to *both* the *victorious* and the *vanquished*. They *all* are our brothers, fathers, mothers, without distinction of *race, creed* in *religion* or *in politics*. " *The moral in action* " or *religion* if you please, although *for me*, there is an *Ocean!* of difference between *both*, but for many it is probably *synonymous*, so we are *all right* in our intentions *only* we *differ* in our ways of worshipping God! or going to Heaven! This is only an affair of æsthetics, as all roads go to Rome! only I think the *straight* line is the *shortest*, don't you?.... " If strong *minded*, charitable people, philanthropists go to Heaven the above lady 'Mrs. Miller' ought to have a double selected seat *there*.

N. B.— I began the above episode on digression or divagation on gardener's and expressman's swindling, and I conclude on *moralizing*. *The extremes meet* — and we progress.... *slowly* in *moral affairs*.

In the period of 1856–58–59, when the Brooklyn Hort. Society, *erat floruit*, was flourishing, I got acquainted with a very sympathetic gentleman in good many ways, but with exceptions. He was very fond of plants, and a refined taste, always with some exceptions; he was enthusiastic and liberal; when he took a fancy to a plant he did not stop for a few cents or dollars. He lived in N. Jersey city; he had a good collection of choice plants, even Orchids, that began to attract attention. He was jealous of my few laurels and told me that he would soon compete against me and meant to distance me. I answered him that it was just what I wanted, I wished, opposition, "as to vanquish without danger was a victory or triumph without glory. I do not recollect the particulars of our first contest. I only remember that we had a prize offered for a single plant for one foliage or variegated plant; he had " Rhopala corlovadensis " and I had "Dioon edule" a Mexican species of Cycadeæ; both we were absent when the prize was awarded; he got second, I got first. That little *skirmish* seemed to disturb his equanimity, for when we met he asked me if I did not think the judges had made a mistake; that his plant was the *best*. I told him I could not help it, to ask the judges and perhaps they would rectify their mistake. Well, he said, you know better; perhaps I do, but even so, I am not a judge; I cannot alter their decision. Both plants were new and had never been exhibited before. He said his plant was newer; both had been imported from England and Belgium; he said his plant was more valuable, he had paid £2. I told him mine cost me £5 (was not that a silly dialogue for two seemingly sensible men ?) The current of events went on, and came another Exhibition; we

competed for six *Variegated* plants, and he competed
for one Single Variegated with somebody else. He
defeated me for six, but got beaten for one single plant,
and that exasperated him; he was furious all that
day; he waited until evening to see me, to have my
opinion, and when arrived at the Athenæum building,
where was the exhibition, he took me with one arm as
a policeman would have taken a pick-pocket caught
in flagrante delicto, and told me come! I will show *you*
what *your* judges have done! We were in front of
the table where the plants stood, and a crowd discussing
about the award. He said: Here is a man for whom I
care more than all of you, a judge of plants; if he says
you have acted right when you gave me the *second*
premium, I will confess I am wrong. They had taken
off the labels so I could not see which was first or
second; I did not want it. During all these preliminaries
I stood stern and grave as Solomon, when he decided
between the two mothers. They asked me which was
the best plant; I put my finger on the Anœchtochilus,
I now forget the specific name, it had golden leaves,
it was a pretty plant, it had the 2d prize, Caladium.
Caladium Chantini the 1st, the 2d prize was his plant.
When he heard my decision he said: It is all right now,
I know what I wanted to know, so saying, he went
out. Here I see that I have made a *lapsus*, after hearing
that *C. Chantini* had the 1st prize; I asked who were

the *asses* who had awarded the premiums? The chairman of the committee who was behind me, pulled by a sudden jerk the skirt of my coat, so as to say, *keep your tongue*, but it was too late, so I uttered again the same expression, so that the audience could see I did not want any misunderstanding; that chairman was a nice quiet man, a German gardener — a florist of Brooklyn, called Rauch; he had a great knowledge of plants, he was well educated, but he was too fond of PLEASURE!! and his income did not permit him to *cultivate* such a *common plant*, but *expensive* to grow in *specimen!!* In that circumstance he was what the French call "Tirer le Diable par la queue," "Pulling the Devil by his tail," to be *hard up;* that is to say, not *independent*. Our *owner* of the *Anœchtochilus* was gone, but the litigation about the awards of the two plants was not settled yet; after our owner of Anœchtochilus was gone the chairman of the committee tried to justify himself. He said: Mr. Menand! you have been *too rash* in your decision; had you known the whole affair you would not have talked as you did. We gave the 1st prize to the Caladium because we found out that the *Anœchtochilus* was not his plant, he had *borrowed* it from *Mr. P.*, *his friend*, a few days before the exhibition. Well, my friend! Your justification is *worse* than your *fault.* If you had found — discovered the trick you ought not to award him any prize at all, but have him *disqualified!* He would probably have done it but he *durst not.* You understand the reason? that gentleman *Borrower of plants* as I have said, was a liberal man and as I understood very willing to oblige his friends, and our chairman was deeply under obligations to him. Hence the *award*, jumping from the frying pan into the fire.—But it seemed that they had not discovered the whole series of tricks used at that exhibition. In the lot of six variegated or foliage plants exhibited against me there were *two* that came from the same place at the *Anœchtochilus!* The owner afterward confessed to me that it was a *mean trick* and would never do it again. In the morning, after all our plants were arranged on the table, I gave a look over the whole exhibit, and I thought I knew some of the plants as *not belonging* to the man who had them exhibited, but of course it never occurred to me that either of those two men would resort to such mean tricks, for both men appeared to me as gentlemen, *one, at least*, as any, farther I can not tell, both men were *intimate friends?* — as it is generally understood, but the *Lender* was a *subaltern* to the *Borrower* and you know! "Borrowing dulls the edge of husbandry" and also the edge of friendship in the occasion!!

Both of those friends had shown me a great deal of

deference in many ways, notwithstanding our divergence of opinion in many things.

Later, in the course of horticultural events, etc., I had some difficulty with one of them, even with both. Yet, if this day I had any trifling influence in the Celestial Regions, to open to them the gates of the kingdom of Heaven, I would do it, although I do not know what has become of them since that time.

From that exhibition of *good* plants and *dirty* tricks, our Amateur No. 1st had resolved in his liberal mood and *sub-wisdom* to have a special premium, "*to be offered*" by the Brooklyn Hort. Society to the best collection of all kinds of plants, foliage, or flowering plants, which *had never been exhibited in America*. That prize to be a large silver pitcher and half dozen goblets of the same metal, worth $500 *or* $600 !..... He was willing it seemed *to pay for*, but, with the understanding it would be awarded to him. A meeting to that effect was held in Jersey City, I think in his own residence, I am not positive, having lost the document that my informant, Mr. Alexander Gordon, gardener to Mr. Hoyt of Astoria, L. I., had given me of the proceedings of the meeting. My friend A. Gordon had been delegated by the Brooklyn Hort. Society. After the reading of the resolution he rose and said, Mr. V. W.: I understand that you want to offer a premium which "you will pay for" and take a mortgage on our *Bona fide.* Willingness to support your *scheme!* that's plain English, and, We, I understand, shall have to compete against you, with our *pennies* against your *dollars?* That " Gordian Knot " can not be *untied* by any one of us, our *spades* are not *sharp* enough to cut it, and we *have not "Alexander's"* (the great) sword to cut it, unless it be *mine!!* Alex. Gordon and I am not willing to lend nor send it neither to our Hort. Soc. nor any body else.

That practical oration closed the meeting. The day after my friend sent me an abridged account of the proceeding, and I immediately wrote to our *Lender* of plants of what I knew about the Premium Silver Goblet and Pitcher that was to be awarded at our next exhibition in Brooklyn. I told him that I had made up my mind, and I was preparing my energy for the contest, and that I was confident to annihilate the "Jersey Blues" and bring the Pitcher and silver goblets to Albany, and that when they would visit Albany, and the Albany *Dutchman,* I could treat them with Albany *ale* (then *famous*) served up in those goblets, etc. When in my vein of joking I think I made some allusions to our " *Borrower No.* 1," whom I supposed was a " Centurion " in the legion of "Jersey Blues." That letter was private, but somehow or another it fell in the hands of the "Centurion," Borrower No. 1, by the agency of the Lender, *No.* 2. Some explanations were given to me about that *diminutive scandal*, but I did not believe a word of it. However, a few days after my onslaught on our "Centurion" I received from him a letter of four pages of the size I write these *historical divagations*, of close writings of *abuse* rather *silly*, and the man *was not* a fool, but his pride had been wounded. He began his letter by "Here inclosed my check for $50, amount of bill rendered to me for plant *wrongly labelled*," etc., etc. So you can see he *was honest*. I liked that sort of exordium, but his long *epistle*, and its longer and more abusive and silly *peroration*, made me *mad first*, then I laughed with pity for I had a *foible* for him. Nine-tenths of his letter, if not *all*, was the most elaborate theme of *Billingsgate rhetoric* I have seen. He evidently had made up his mind to make the letter as long as he could, and *I resolved* to make my answer as short as possible. In that letter he threatened me to send me one like it every week. He never did it. It seemed he had told his friend he would do so. The friend told him not to send it to me, and if I should answer it, he would be sorry—I know Menand. When he got my answer, you will see below, he went to show it to him. He frankly told his friend he was sorry, *but too late*.

I cannot remember that letter. His letter, and my answer to it, I kept it for a few years. Then I destroyed *both*, fearing that perhaps later I would be tempted to make use of it, and be sorry after.

MR. V. W.:

Dear Sir: Thanks for your check; receipt inclosed. I have received your theme of Billingsgate rhetoric. I have had some trouble to understand it, as I do not profess the English Belles-Lettres as you do. For instance, you tell me I *do not like* you because you have never treated me with *a gin-cocked-tail*. Well, sir, I did not know what it meant, but a friend of mine tells me that if I want to know the meaning of it, I must go to *the school* where you have learned your *Belles-Lettres*, that is to say, with the company you associate with, viz: Blacklegs, pugilists, cockfighters, rowdies of all sorts. Yours,

L. MENAND.

P. S.—The above letter, short as it is, is twice as long as the one I wrote at that date — 1858-9 ? My vein is too *old* to-day, I cannot recollect.

Those who may have read my above lucubrations will probably think I have done with my *often far-fetched* prose. Remember: at the beginning of these reminiscences I have said that my weak point was not *lacon-*

ism. So you must expect some little disappointment; after all, you know "the saying "There is no rose without thorns" and if any spines on my productions they are not as prickly as those of our *modern Rose growers*, and do not cost as much as your "American Beauties," and mine, not *roses*, but my productions "or flowers of rhetorics," will last *longer* even in a *warm* place, that is to be taken in consideration. All these few words are to let you know that I have more to say about my or *our* Amateurs — *Lender* and *Borrowers* of plants. After our exchange of amenities of *the four pages* of *Billingsgate* and my answer to it. We had a *truce!* even *peace* — without laying down our weapons, that is to say in plain English, without ceasing to grow plants with which *we* had fought for the sake of *glorious Vanity*. I said we had peace; my opponent after a while, when he cooled off, thought we had been foolish, and one day he came hither to our headquarters with the *Olive* branch, by *intuition* — we *shook* hands, and the peace was signed. Still, the man had always some of his tricky notions, though inoffensive, *bad habit* only. We looked all over our plants, new and old, it was the time we had the monomania of getting new plants *often* not worth the water they drank. I had several plants he had never seen as Latania aurea, Latania rubra, Thrinax argentea, etc. He did not know the *names* and *wanted* badly to *know*

them, but he did not wish to ask me *depending* on
my *itching* for *talking* and that I would tell him what
he wanted to know *without asking*, but by that time
I had made some progress in the study of the " *human
heart*," and I *guessed!* by his looks what was ferment-
ing in his *brains* and I acted accordingly. I made up
my mind he would not know one single name unless
he should ask me twice or more. I suppose we went
three times to and fro to look at all the plants he wished
to know. It is rather tedious to use so many words for
such a trifle, but I want to edify you whether you will
or not, *nolens-volens*. I had (a variegated plant) a
variety of a common English weed *Coltsfoot*. It looked
very pretty as it was; he saw it *although* it was somewhat out of the way. He said first, it is very pretty.
"John *has it too*." Do you know who was *John?* No!
nor I either, but I *guessed*, I like to guess, especially
when I am *sure*, the second time he passed by he said
that plant *will take* in New York, but no progress had
been done in getting the name. I was dumb as a snail
and I did not draw my horns; the third time he said:
could you *spare me one*, and what-do-you-call-it? Well,
I thought you told me *John had it?* If so it would be
a great deal better to get it from him, I have not many.
Well, he said, I would rather get it from you, send *me*
one with the other plants I have selected. Yes, I will do
it. Then I told him: What the devil possessed you

to hesitate so much to ask after names. Do you think because a man knows more names of any thing he is better than one who does not? Certes, it is a satisfaction to know the names of the objects you *have*, but I don't see the necessity to be so mysterious. A few more digressions on that *not bad man* but *ill-balanced*. He once had asked me a list of the *most* remarkable plants I had seen, new or old, and also to his lender of plants. Both wanted something the other had not, that I understood it....it was a *laudable idea*. I gave a list to both of about the same plants, but unknown to each other. Some weeks or months after, I now forget, I met them in New York. They would not let me go unless I should go with them to Jersey city, to see some new plants they had just received from London. I was not very willing to go, but the Borrower insisted so much, and the Lender also, and in addition to my desire to see something that I had never seen, that I went. I expected they would talk again about our correspondence, but not a word was spoken on that scabrous subject. We were hardly in the office of the "Silver pitcher's originator," that he went in an adjoining room *and came* with a *basket* of *champagne*. At that time champagne was still imported in willow baskets. The moment I saw it, it produced *on me* a sudden commotion in all my body that I cannot describe. My sensation then was *surely* a *vivid pleasure* and a *wonderful* amount of surprise mingled with all. I cannot find an expression to render what I felt. The famous "*gin-cocked-tail*" came to my mind at once, and I was already comparing the two liquors together. The most *aristocratic* with the most *demagogic!* Do you realize earnestly the idea to offer me *champagne* after that *anarchist gin-cocked-tail*. I had not fully recovered my presence of mind — my wits, when the wine was in the cups, when he raised his glass and said to the health of our Americanized friend, L. M.!! Do you think that was an *apology* for the insults he had thrown in my face when he was *unconscious* of his doings? In that *moment* I would not have exchanged it for the whole world. When we had drunk the contents of the bottle we went to see the new plants. With new sensations .... but with our SAME feelings of old, "Lupus pilum mutat, non mentem." "The wolf changes its coat but not its character."

When we came in presence of the group of newly imported plants, I, with *reverence* — admiration — surprise, took off my hat, and looked at the owner of the plants, and the plants also, while he did the same, observing the *external* change of my feelings on my face — to find what they could be internally; he could see my surprise in my eyes *fixed* on the plants, but I could also see in his countenance, he was literally palpitating with exultation, bliss, joy, to find he had something I did not know or not seen; in a few seconds of mutual contemplation, I exclaimed: Where have you found those plants?! You must have had trouble to get them, and you must have paid a good price for them, for they are, as far as I know, rare and difficult to have, even with money. Then he was to the apogee of his happiness! But it did not last long, for he asked me, have you ever seen any of them? Do you know the names of any? *Quietly* as it becomes a man, an actor, if you please, who knows his part, I said yes, I know some of them, not all. Well, then, tell me? What is this? What is that? I looked at him, and told him. Why! Mr. ———, you must have a very short memory! Do you not recollect some time ago you asked me if I would not give you a list of the best, rarest, newest and most remarkable plants, old or new, I had seen? He kept silent for a few seconds, then said: Tell me the names! Instantly as a horse which feels the spur, I told him, here is Latania rubra, Thrinax radiata, Cossignia borbonica gone *ad patres*, dead, this I have never seen but once, 35 years since, this I only knew the name, but could apply it. In a great deal less time than it has taken me to write these names, that, his arms, which rested on his *haunches* dropped on his *thighs*, with a change in his countenance really alarming for any one not knowing the cause. In that moment if he had translated his feelings in words, he would have said : What is the use to get pains, spend money to show that Franco-American, that we can get new plants as well as he does. It really pained me to see him so much affected for such a trifle, but such was his temper. All I have here related to you happened 32 or 33 years ago, and "As to-day," "As in the time past," and "As in the future," "We are," "We have been," and "We shall be," susceptible, apt, to appreciate, the "Worthy," and the "Unworthy," the "Sublime and the Base," in *cents* and *dollars* so to day. I would willingly give $100 to shake hands with *that man* if he is alive. This is my sincere desire — wish. If he is dead, this is my *memorial*, "*requiescito* in *pace!*

Rest thou in peace !   Thy friend, L. M.

APPENDIX

OF RETROSPECTIVE RECOLLECTIONS, MISCELLANEOUS, OMITTED OR FORGOTTEN IN THE RECOLLECTIONS PROPER, CONTAINING ALL I HAVE WRITTEN SUBSEQUENTLY — AS FACTS AND INCIDENTS CAME TO MY MEMORY, WITHOUT ANY CHRONOLOGICAL ORDER.

Here a few necessary remarks. When I came to the decision to write my recollections it was with much hesitation, though my children, seeing my deep sorrow after the death of their mother, insisted persistingly, telling me to write the history of plant as I had often spoken of doing, or a sketch of my life from my youngest days to this day, that such occupation would absorb my gloomy thoughts and relieve my mental troubles, and give me some gratification in reviving incidents that happened 75 years ago or more. My souvenirs extend beyond 1814–15 to have seen the debris of that *Waterloo butchery!*....

Meanwhile I accidentally came acquainted with the American Florist Co., Chicago, who solicited me to give them a few sketches of my life connected with horticultural affairs, as a man and gardener. As I have said above I hesitated, fearing with potent reasons to undertake a task above my capacities, knowing my peculiarities not well-balanced for such a work, with my *prime leaping* tendencies to skip over a letter in a word, or words in a phrase, besides I had an idea that those sketches were to be short and concise, two qualities I am deprived of; but amply gifted of two opposed defects, *prolixity* and *digressions* at loss of sight. But I found that I was laboring under a mistake, that it was necessary to give the full understanding of what I was at the age 8 or 10 to 20 or more, to compare what I am at 85, the age of a *young* patriarch, as for the old ones I do not think I shall never *attain* the age of *biblical* Abraham, and I do not wish it even if I was to have an *Agar* for helpmate when 175 years old, I could not forget my Phanerogyne of the old times, besides I am not constituted like Abraham was....

By dint of speaking of religious creed, Heaven and its antipode Hell, priests, etc., it has reminded me of an incident that happened nearly half a century ago. An individual, with whom I was slightly acquainted, told me that he had met *a man* who knew *me* well who had told him that I was a *knowing!* one, that I had studied to be a *priest!* You hear a *priest!* Good God! if never since I was born, any body had studied any more than I had to be enlisted in that corporation there would be nobody to-day, to besot the simpletons except those older than I am, and I suppose the number is limited to-day. God have pity for me, I have never meant to descend to that level.... although I think of it, when I was 10 or 12 years old, I heard an old woman telling my mother that one sister of her (my mother) had told her that if I would study to be a *priest* she would give all she had, and all she would be able to save as long as she *lived* to pay for my education in a Seminary. Was not that a strange coincidence? that a man I hardly knew should know such a circumstance, when myself I had forgotten it.

One thing brings another. I recollect that my father, speaking of that aunt of mine, said one day to somebody who wanted to marry her for her *money*, that "she was pickled in holy water." She died a maid, and I think I must have had some of her money, for she died before my mother and sister, and they were heirs to her, and both my mother and sister died during the Secession War, and that I received from France, through a notary public, some $800, paid in gold, which at that time was worth $1,000. So you see the caprices of Destiny! She wanted to give her money to make a *saint!* and she made a *heretic* her *heir*. However, if any body go to Heaven those *two sisters* ought to go!!....

As I am making my confession, I will make it complete without jesuitic restrictions: I was 18 years, or about, after my father's death; my mother, a *Saint* "in bona fide" when *out* of the *presence*, or of the *influence*, occult, of the *priest*, but when immediately after that *odious auricular* confession, she was.... You will excuse me not to qualify my mother!! I am not a *priest*. I leave to the Supreme —"*unknown*" judge, what that *saint* was. Suffice to say, it was the *holy Thursday*. I had as much to do in one day, as two men would have done in two days. She scolded me for not going to a religious ceremony. I told her that I had too much to do, I could not do it.... Well, she said: My child! I shall be *damned*, and you too! for I am responsible for your soul and mine.... After that admonition of my poor minded mother, I felt — I cannot attempt to describe it to you. I know no English words that would give you an adequate idea of my moral *excruciating* pain.... you understand, *my mother!!* telling me I would be the cause of her *damnation!!*.... for a few seconds I could not speak, I felt paralyzed; when I spoke, I said,

"No! no! mother, there will be no damnation.
"If any, it will be for the hearer of your confession!

When I recovered from my stupor I told her with a tremulous voice, but with a strong determination:

Mother!! If I-knew-the-*wretch* who-has-confessed-you,-advised you-I would-go-this-minute-and *strangle him*, if able to do it.... She weeped bitterly, and I did not feel any better, if not *worse*; she wept with *grief!* and I was *choking with rage!!*.... O! malediction! on the *inventors* of that *odious confession!* After that semi-dramatic scene, I remained about two years longer with my mother and sister, but we had no more quarrels, if she spoke about religion I listened to her, I made no remarks, I answered by monosyllables, yes! or no! or very well! We had what we say in French, "*Put water in our wine,*" that is to say, every one of us tried not to hurt the other's feelings, so we had *a truce*, if not absolutely peace. Now readers, if any, allow me if you please, not to think I have been too impulsive, too exalted in my demonstrations to confess to you in writing to your eyes, not to your ears alone, *not auricular.* That in writing the above episode, I have shed as many tears than there are words in it, in this outburst of my indignation. "In 1825, 66 years ago!"

After I had left my mother and sister in 1827, I went to see them again in 1835. We had been corresponding all the time. My mother was always the same, but we did not have any harsh expressions to exchange. I knew it was probably the last time we would see each other, so I did not tell them I had made up my mind to leave France, where I was called a heretic and blood drinker. I wrote to them after I got settled in Astoria, and a few years after we were settled in Albany. I sent them our Photographs of all of us, nearly *one dozen ! !* as specimens of — *prolific!* America! Since, I have only seen France once, *in* 1878 ; and only from Dieppe to Paris. I have not been to the city where I was born, where I would not have known anybody (43 years), and I was not an "*American uncle,*" and nobody would have recognized me. I was to go, but I missed a train I wanted to go by; I had to wait three hours for another, then I made reflections *so sad! that* I gave it up.

I do admire "France." She has produced that "*colossal!* that "*immense*" revolution of 1789! whose revolutionary commotions have *shaken morally* the whole civilized world. She has compelled *all* the *Potentates* of Europe (England excepted ; she is a *grand nation* also) to pass under the " Furcæ Caudines," i. e., the *yoke* of the *revolutionary patriotic and emancipatory genius* of France ! and that during many years, until her "*first evil* genius " Napoleon I caused her to be *twice invaded* in *one year ;* and, many years later, her " *second superimus evil scoundrel genius* Napoleon III, had her *drowned* in an *ocean* of *ignominy*.... To all these *calamities* France can say "Mea Culpa" "Maxima Culpa.". By so doing she will somewhat *attenuate* her wrongs, for her fondness of *vain glory*. They have given you a "quantum sufficit" of glory your *uncle* and his worthy nephew *Two Emperors* one after the other, is it not glorious? and cheap above all, only for the *bagatelle* of *two provinces!* it is for nothing except *mountains* of *shame!*....that will not be *levelled* down as quickly as they have been created.... unless the *French clergy*, who this day show *so much sympathy* for the *French republic* should settle them down by dint of *holy water irrigations*, it might perhaps make the ground more fertile? God! knows we don't.... France has produced a great many eminent men of genius in all the ramifications of human intelligence.... This *country* of *Uncle Sam* has produced ONE, especially, *Franklin!* put him in the scale, *weigh* his *merits* and compare him to any of the great men of *any country* and draw your conclusions...... mine are drawn if *Yankeedom* should not, over-*weigh* "overbalanced" them all, I would jump in the scales so that she could do it.

When I began to write some of these sketches of my life I meant to relate only the most interesting incidents, but as I proceeded I found that I had omitted many and some I had entirely overlooked, forgotten, and some very typical ones, connected with *wisdom* versus stupidity, and perhaps vice versa. Does not this expression sound odd, queer on my lips! "*confessions?*" It does if you take it to the *letter*, and with its religious meaning, but that confession shall not be *snatched* from me by any *priest* of any denomination whatever, it will be between us, between the whole community, and if it chance not to meet your approbation, you need not give me the *absolution*, and I promise you that I shall not be angry with you for your intolerance, on condition you will not either bear me any malice for what I may say to clear my conscience, to have *sinned* in the eyes of some, but *not* in mine, for it may happen that what one of us calls *virtue* I may consider it as a *venial* vice.... Now that I have done my introductory prayer, let us begin: In 1827 I was only between 19 and 20 years old, half between the *two*. I lived in one of the suburbs of Paris, within a few hundred yards of the city walls, *intra muros* (within the walls), but I boarded *extra muros* (outside the walls), so as not to pay *double* price for wine, when I *drank* any, for I did not care much for it at that time, but necessity *compelled* me not to, yet I had to do it on account of the water *not agreeing* with new comers. A bottle of wine that cost 16 *cents in Paris* cost only 8 *cents outside* owing to city duties, and when a man gets 50 *francs* ($10) a month he cannot very well afford to drink wine, but I had to do it and board myself, it was a question of *hygiene* and I could *not afford* to be sick ....

Let us come to the *psychologic incident*. I had a comrade 8 or 10 years my senior, not exactly a Parisian but born in the jurisdiction of Paris, he was a sort of *philosopher!* as you will see. It was on what you call in English "Good Friday." We went to our boarding house, where there were perhaps 30 or more people, all mechanics of different trades. We were the only two exceptions, in trade, and in principles; almost uniformly every one had beef soup, and after soup (soup and a Frenchman are almost synonymous), boiled beef and vegetables at your option. One word before we go further. After we were all sat down and waiting for the waiters I gave a glance all over the company (I already began to study human kind) to see how all those philosophers were going to "*feed*" — excuse me this word, it answers my purpose. I found that the majority ordered *beef soup*. I might say the whole. After soup the waiter asked us what we wanted. I don't know what he asked others. I had seen the *soup served up*. That was all I wanted for my *edification*, but I was mistaken. I had only seen one-half of the performance, the waiter came to me and asked me in a whisper what do you want? I told him *beef* and mashed potatoes. He brought it to me and at once I began to put half of my beef in my *loaf* of *bread* for my dinner, as it was the custom then, it cost less to buy it from the baker than from the restaurant, then I began to eat the balance left. When my *comrade*, who stood opposite me, *rose from his chair, crossed his arms over* his breast and *thrust* in my face these "flowers of rhetoric" (we were *florists* and of course that was one of our weapons): "D.... savage! *double brute!!* have you been brought up with *wild beasts!* in the woods where you *ought to be* and not among *civilized? people!!*....to eat meat on such day!!.... After that complimentary apostrophe, allocution as you please, the utterance of which seemed to have exhausted all his faculties, he could hardly draw his breath, he was *panting!* and I was *suffocating! with rage*, with all the most violent passions in a human body. At that minute, that second, from a *roaring* in the room you could have heard the flying of an *atom*, a silence like in a tomb! So spontaneous had been the *frantic* allocution, every one was surprised and I was *petrified!* as to say. If at that time the terrestrial globe had had a handle through it and I could have handled it as my spade I would have rolled it over *all* in existence, crushing to dust every thing, then you would have had a cause to say to-day "*dust to dust!* But I don't think I said any thing *at all*, unless internally

"Infernal stupid fools, beastly bipeds, you ought to eat *hay* instead of *bread.*"

Much ado about nothing some one might say! Yes it was *something!* and the *morality* of it would have been this: If that beastly man had been able to *strangle me* as his disposition appeared to be, nobody would have interfered in my behalf, for in my honest conviction they had the same ideas more or less, for *not one* expressed his *indignity* of the insult *to me*, and in such case you know the old saying "who says nothing consents."

To end that confession, I will tell all my sins in that fanatical strife was, that when that man addressed me I thought from his look that he was to leap over the table and take me by the neck. I had my hand on a decanter half full of water, and if he had jumped or turned round the table and touched me I would have smashed it on his head, unless he had been the strongest, and to-day, after over 64 years, I still believe nobody would have interfered, though *probably* none would have helped him, but....

Now, I would like to ask those who may have read the first part of my biography, what they think of that incident "*eating boiled beef*" on a *Good Friday*, or any other Friday, after other persons *would have eaten* the *essence of it?* And then call that *beef eater* a *double brute*, etc., and thinking he, the *Beefophagus* will go *to hell* for the crime of having eaten what you had *sucked*, and he who *had absorbed* the *juice* of that beef will go to *Heaven!* Is not that a wonderfully pious action? One can go to heaven cheaply. Probably there are some persons who would tell me that that was only an *isolated case*, but *unfortunately not*, it is the *rule*, not the exception. Long before that, I had seen almost as bad in a different way. When, one, as *I*, have seen such acts of *fanaticism*, in a city like *Paris!* when this *very day* the *French nation* hesitates to have a separation of the State from that *clerical breed!* whose majority, to-day, *would*, if they had the *power*, *proclaim* a new "Saint *Bartholomew*" of all who would *not believe*, that *confession* is an *ignominious* — an *infamous* institution, to *degrade* human species .... to corrupt *young people*, especially the *feminine* sex. I wish that in this paper I am writing on I could with *decency unveil* your *turpitudes*, but we cannot dispose of a *confessional* as you do. We have to observe decency .... It makes my blood *boil* when I think there are men that *teach* you you will go to Hell in eating meat on certain days — or in not believing that they are the *ministers* of *God!* O! Impostors! O! French Philosophers!.

An incident in my life, in 1838, in Astoria, L. I., N. Y.—Expelled out of the railroad cars for want of ten cents change, with forty dollars bills of good money.

In March, 1838, I had been in the employ of Mr. Geo. Thorburn, of New York, on his place, at Astoria, since 1st of October, 1837, and by that time I had not received one cent—having no need of money I had not asked for, as I had a few dollars in reserve, but to try my proficiency in writing English, for as speaking it tolerably I was backward. So I wrote to him that I should like a few dollars, if convenient. The very same day he sent me $40 in bank bills, all single dollar bills, and probably of forty different banks of New York State, but not of New York city. Those forty dollars were such dirty looking in appearance, that if they had been spread over the pavement in the street, I would not have stooped down to pick them up. True, I knew nothing about the money. The following day was a Sunday. I decided to go to New York, so I went to the Hell Gate ferry to cross the river, thence went to Yorkville to take the steam cars to go to the city. Yorkville was the *terminus* of the railroad. The tunnel between Yorkville and Harlem was not finished then. There was no station for the railroad, but close to the stairway to go down to get into the cars there was a saloon, or a tavern, and I went in, not willing to wait in the open air, as it was drizzling, snowing and cold, but I thought it was not proper to stand in such place without taking something, so I asked for "*a glass* of *beer,*" only those *four* words. I must have pronounced them in a queer way, or the bar-tender was dull enough. Anyhow he took a small bottle (the contents of which did not look like beer to me) and filled up a large glass. I took the glass with one hand and handed a silver coin with the other. I forgot if it was 10 cents or more or less, I think it was Spanish or Mexican money. He took it and did not give me any change. I tasted the *would*-be-beer but I could not drink it. It was as bitter as *Aloe* to my taste, so I put my glass on the bar again, and all the time he looked at me but I did not say a word nor he either, but from his *look*, if he had *spoken*, I think he would have said: "What sort of a fool are you? You ask for a drink, you pay for it and you do not drink it, nor say a word whether you find it bad or not. I would have asked but I could not manage to find words to ask him what sort of medicine he had given me. The train had arrived so I went down and got in the car. I do not think there was *more* than one person and myself in the car. In a few minutes the conductor came and asked me my fare without speaking, I could understand his pantomime, so I handed him one dollar bill of those dirty looking bills. He looked at it, shook his head and stood looking at me with some impatience. I gave him another, then he said *no good.* I could understand that without an *interpreter.* I gave him another from the same bundle I had in my coat pocket. Same ceremony. He would not take it and began to wax mad and put his hand on my shoulder to turn me out, but I was not willing to go. It began to snow pretty heavy. I held the seat I was sitting on with one hand and with the other one I pulled my bundle of bills and I gave it to help himself, but he still held *me* and wanted to drag me out. I think he had succeeded to push me a few yards but by that time the gentleman who was in the car took his arm from me. Then they began to discuss rather lively and quarrel. I could not understand what they said but I could understand the gestures of both, and that the gentleman who interfered in my behalf was telling that man I was not a swindler, and that all those bills I had offered him were good. The result of that incident was I went *free.* When we arrived, I think 28th street, I thanked the gentleman the best I could and went down to the post-office to see if I had a letter from France that I expected. A clerk who talked French and English told me there were two. He handed them to me. I took them and gave him one of those dollars. He looked at it and told me "I cannot take that bill. Why? I said is it bad? No it is good, but we do not take any bank bill unless *New York city* bills or silver. He took back my two letters and gave me my dollar. Then I said what shall I do. Well he said go to that Jew clothing-store and buy a vest or any thing else, give your bills and they will give you change. I told him I wanted nothing at all. Well go into the tavern close by and take a glass of *beer*. The *devil* with the *beer*. I thought of the glass I had had at Yorkville, but as I could not get change any other way I did take it and got the change of my dollar. The change *was* about as *bright* as the bills, some *six cents, one shilling*. That most of them looked like little rounds of TIN. You could hardly see any thing on them so much worn out by long handling. The same night when I got back to Astoria I wrote again to Mr. Thorburn to whom I recounted my trouble. He told me to send back the money (bills) and he would send me silver *American coin.*

He did not send me silver, but quite *new bank bills* of New York city. But, as the proverb has it "a burnt child dreads the fire," I felt in doubt, and I was much puzzled where to go to test their intrinsic value. There was only one grocery in the village, as far as I knew, and I did not want to buy any thing at all. I might have asked for a glass of beer, but I had enough of it. I was afraid it would be from the same brewery I drank at Yorkville, so I asked for a *candle!* A candle? Yes. You may laugh, for when I got out of the store, going back to my lodging, I laughed myself at my shrewdness! We *burned* oil, and I had no need of it. I laughed a great deal more than *all those* who may read this *silly story* will, for after lighting my *flambeau* I took a book to read, to see if it was good tallow or wax, and the first thing I read, was, a story of a fellow of my *school* who went to a dry good store and walked from one end to the other of the store, when one of the clerks asked him what he wanted? O! nothing, he said, I only wanted to see the *store keeper's daughter*, and I do not see her, is she gone out? The story did not say if he wanted to buy her, as I had done, with my candle.... But that incident of being turned out of railroad cars for want of ten cents, when I had forty dollars in my pocket, did not give me a very good opinion of American money, for many years later the country was literally overflooded with such dirty money, and to help it, quantities of those bills counterfeited. When you went in a store to buy for sixpence, if you had no small change to pay for, you had to wait ten or fifteen minutes, until the storekeeper had looked in a sort of detector to see if your money was good. That was not the *Golden Age!!*

Appendix.

Specimen of Brutality.

Speaking of grandeur versus littleness, reminds me of a circumstance. In 1841, three countrymen of mine, two living in New York, and one in Albany, came to pay me a visit in Astoria. One of them, a splendid, tall looking man (physically speaking) one of the debris of the Waterloo's cataclysm of blood, asked me if I was a married man? I answered affirmatively. Married to an American lady or a French one? I replied an English one. English? Yes! Well he said with a *wry face*, she loses seventy-five per cent in my estimation!! Sir, I believe you, since you say so, but *I*, in my appreciation of your *high stature*, and *narrow-minded idea*, I think....that you....are an *ass!* He changed color at hearing that apostrophe, and made a motion of his right arm, as I made of my right foot "to shake the kinkles out o' back an' leg, an o' rack my face off from a *filip*, I thought he was going to administer me. But suddenly one of his friends, the Albanian, another debris of the catastrophe of Waterloo, threw his arms across the body of that *appraiser* of a woman he had never seen, and of a man he saw for the first time, and told him : Rioux! (I think it was his name) it is a shame for you to insult a man, and a woman you have never seen, and do not know any thing about him or her. If you *touch* him you will have to knock me down first, and be sorry after. And he would have been sorry, for my foot and leg were braced to give him a *filip* on his *lower abdomen*. I had no other weapon, and I could not grapple with such a colossus. His weight alone could have crushed me, although, I was not *lame* at that time. But " all is well that ends well.".... Only I should like to make some commentaries on such a man — one of those *satellites* of the *uncle* of his *nephew*, brave on the battle-field, but, otherwise, most of the time reasoning as a *horse!!* Can you understand that illogical, semi-brute expressing himself against a woman, who had more sense *in her fingers* (queer comparison, but it suits my meaning) than he had in his whole individual, to *hate* any one, because born in a certain country! That man ought to have admired *the English* for he had seen them *face* to *face* on that "*Abattoir! of human bodies*, Waterloo! If that *man* had had *a grain* of common sense he would have looked with *respect* — with *profound admiration*, at the sight of " Wellington," surrounded or with his aides-de-camp, Lords Hill and Gordon, already killed : " General, if you expose yourself to *be killed*, what shall we do? As *I do—to be killed!* was his answer. A *grand*, a *noble* answer!! *For me* that day Wellington was greater than Napoleon. I shall not qualify this last — *decency forbids me*....

APPENDIX.

But, here, I cannot refrain from making reflections on the blindness, prejudices, irrational insane ideas of nation against nation. Why those hatred, inveterate feelings between two nations, France and England, especially?.... Who will answer those arduous questions? Neither of them collectively! "L'Amour propre Français" on one side, and the "English Pride" on the other side, and *both* together, will, I am afraid, prevent forever an *union* between them. That "amour propre Français," that I incline to render it, by "Amour *sale — bête — dirty, foolish*, and the English pride by English "*arrant nonsensicalness*," are monstrous anomalies, which ought to make *both blush* with *shame*, if they should take the thing in earnest consideration? Inasmuch as I have the profound conviction that *both*, individually, not collectively, *unfortunately* have among them, men who think for themselves, who have *admiration* for each other nation, but will not *confess* it — not to the ears of a priest. I do not want such a confession. I wish it " *Coram in ore omnibus orbe,*" " In face of the whole *world!* "

If these two nations would *clasp hands* with each other " sans arrière pensée," " without any "moral restrictions." They, even to-day, at the *dawn* of the *twentieth century!* they could have the *pre-eminence* over the whole of *Europe!* if not more .... That is my ardent wish, and I would like to see it before I take my exit.... But what *seas* of difficulties in the way, impediments of all sorts : difference of *language,* foremost, *religious creed* next, and probably, as bad, if not worse, rivalry, jealousies among all classes of society, etc., etc.... I think, from the reflections I make in *sketching* that *dream,* it will be as well for me to take my *exit* as soon as the doors will be open and not waste my *illusions,* though they do not cost me much, yet *it is a pity* not.... not to see that *dream* a reality .... These *illusions* of mine in reference to an *union* between France and England have been nursed up in my bosom for the last fifty years, and more! but the prospect is that I shall die with them unrealized.... it is a pity!!

L. M.

In April, 1831, as I was going to leave Paris, I had omitted to relate the particulars of my engagement, which I had not thought proper to mention, but since I have found it necessary to give an adequate idea of the growing of my principles in religion, politics, moral, intellectual affairs, etc. The *man* of whom I have spoken as a *ferocious royalist* that wanted to *civilize* people with volleys of musketry to prevent the spreading of democratic principles, had recommended me to a gentleman living in Paris most of the time, except 3 or 4 months in Autumn, who wanted a gardener for his mother. I went to see him, and after a little talk, about wages only, for that man who would have *shot me* in the street, had told him to *hire* me with his eyes shut, *closed*, that I was *all right*. As he objected to pay me what I asked, I told him I would take what he used to pay, but if after one or two months he found I was worth more he would pay me what I had asked. At the end of the month his mother paid me what I had stipulated. We had all settled about the day I would leave Paris. When I began to think I had forgotten to ask him if his mother was a religious woman? What makes you ask such a question, he said. I ask that because I know folks in the country are fond of going to church, and I am not! and that probably your mother might require me to go. Oh, yes! he said, she is very strict for that. All right she does what suits her and I want the same privilege. Oh what a fool you are; I don't care for religion, any more than you do, but to please her I do it. It is all right for you, she is your *mother*, but she is not mine! you understand? You act hypocrisy to please her, but I did not wish to do so for my own mother. Well he said I find it is of no use to talk any more about it, but I am sorry. Your appearance, your ways of talking please me, but I see you are determined. Well, I told him I am as sorry as you are, and more so, for I need

employment and you can do without me. I think of
one thing, and if you approve it and if your mother
sanctions it I will go immediately. Write to your
mother, tell her I am a *Protestant*, if she does not object all is settled. Good! you have a luminous idea.
I see that you have more than one string to your bow.
I will write her and I have not the least doubt she will
accept that proposition, when I will tell her that you
suit me. So it was all right — no it was not for a
sudden idea struck me that perhaps when I would be
there among those people, who worshipped a different
God from mine, they would drive me away, stone me,
make a martyr of me, and I have not the ambition to
see my name in a martyrology; as I have already
declined to be a simple *saint!* All the time I was
reciting that tirade he gravely looked at me then burst
with loud laughing. Oh no! they won't do that, they
are not as fanatic as that, you may depend upon it.
On the contrary the few *Protestants* there are more
respected than a great many orthodox sectarians; you
may go safely, so I went, but after I had been there
a few days they tried to submit me at the diet of
spinage on *Fridays* and *Saturdays*. I *winced* at that
violation of our convention, signed by both parties,
etc., etc. I had a good deal *of fun* and occasionally I
waxed mad, but I soon got over it, especially when
the gentleman who had engaged me was present. We

had a good deal of fun with religious farces. We even made alterations in the calendar. We used to call Fridays and Saturdays " the first and the second days of spinages, the other days of fast through the year *extra* spinage day. So far as that we agreed but no farther. He was unprincipled, he was what we generally call a *good fellow!* in a restrictive sense. A handsome looking man, high stature. During the Peninsular Spanish war he had been an aide-de-camp of General Duke of Raguse, then *at the time I speak of* he was living on a *pension* from an uncle, a French general, and some other little scraps. When talking politics if you asked him to what party he belonged he answered that *he* leaned on the "woman bosom." He had been a Bonapartiste of course, and he was then a very *lukewarm* Philippist, King Louis Philippe. On the subject of *woman* we often *wrangled* with animation. He was *unscrupulous*, even dissolute, no respect for them, not even for his own *mother*, for several times I assisted at some domestic quarrel between them (mother and son), and I had to interfere in such a way that *once* he told me: *You!* if you were not in my mother's house I would.... What would you do?? compel me to swallow your *rusted* swords, your *panoply* (he had one in a room under mine). You know very well that those antiquities do *not scare* me more than the *proprietor of them!* Do you not recollect *lately* when

I have *saved* you from *killing* your servant or being killed yourself by him? Do you not see yet the *but end* of that musket in my hand *swinging* over your *head* and that of your *drunken* valet? Did I look like one afraid of you? "*Baron!* out of fashion? (he was called a *Baron* and the mother a Baroness). He and that man had a difficulty. The servant was *drunk* and insulted him without any reason whatever. He was sitting eating his dinner when the fellow, *drunk*, went to him and took him by the arm and abusing him. Then the insulted man took a carving knife to stab him, but the fellow was a powerfully strong *man*, stopped his arm but could not snatch the knife from him then. I was coming from my room when I saw all the women in the house screaming in a terrific manner. By that time they had got out of the dining room and where in a large kitchen where there was a large table 10 or 12 or more feet long and 6 inches thick, running up to a mantle piece over which were 2 or 3 fowling pieces. I could not separate them, I would have been crushed between them, both strong men. I jumped on the table, took one of the muskets by the barrel. They were wrestling at the end of the table close by me; *then* I *shouted* if any one of you move one inch either way I smash his head! I had no looking glass to see how I looked, but all the women told me after, that I looked like a *demon*, that my eyes were protruding out of my sockets. All I can tell is that they both looked at *me*. They were still grappling, and I still with my musket in my *hand*. Then for a second or two a dead silence, no screaming. Then I said you *Mr. Baron*, you are a *coward* to take a knife against a *drunken* man *unconscious*, and you, the servant, you are a *brute !* Get out this moment and you give me your knife and go and finish your dinner if you can.... both went out quietly, in *appearance*. The old mother took me in her arms, and the other women. Some of them kissed me. I was a hero, but I felt a little uneasy about my drunken fellow, but I soon found he was no longer drunk. He was quiet *when sober*, and instead of quarreling with me as I thought he would he *thanked* me for my intervention. What made me so terribly mad in that affray is that man had got drunk in my company. We had been in a village feast where he drank with every body, and I was talking and also drinking *as a pretext* to observe the company, good people enough, that enjoyed perhaps *half a dozen* times in the course of the year, and *toiled hard* and lived about the same the 359 other days.

Now let us go back to our Baron, and his panoply. The day after that "Brutum fulmen," "Harmless thunderbolt," he came to me and told me: Louis! I know you were not afraid of me, though you were *trembling*, but I knew it was not fear, but choler, anger, wrath. If I had touched you what would you have done? Please do not ask me such a question, I cannot tell. Yes, I understand that, but I wish to know for my own edification. Well, if you had touched me seriously, with the idea to *hurt* me you would have had to *kill* me or *disabled* me on the spot, or else exchange my conditions for you to be *killed* or unable to *defend* yourself. Then I would have been sorry forever. Well, he said, all is over, and I hope it will not happen any more. Once in a while a quarrel occurred between him and his mother, and I was always mixed in the contest as an arbitrator. I, most of the time, *inclined* on the side of the mother. But, in my conscience, after over sixty years, I am obliged to say that neither were *saints*. Yet both treated me well, the mother especially, notwithstanding her bigotism and *venial weakness*, I had sympathy for her. Often when I came from my herborization loaded with plants, she came and asked me what I had found new during the whole day, from 3 *A. M.* to 4 or 5 *P. M.* Have you been all that time looking for plants? Yes, Madame! Well, she said, you have modified your *love inclinations.* Don't you recollect the first day you came here from Paris you went in the garden with one of my young servants to show you the topography of the place, and the first thing you did *you kissed her* several times! Don't you recollect, I *upbraided* you for having done so, and you asked me who had told me so. I told you some folks working in the vineyards on the hills culminating the garden had seen you, and you answered me as if you had achieved a great feat — that you had done so and would do it again as soon as you would have a chance, if she would permit you. Is it so? Well, Madame, then I wanted to flirt; to "woo in *naturalibus,*" and to-day I do love *platonically.* I try to learn the theory of expressions proper to express my love *when I shall find* the person that shall inspire me. *Love!* as I understand it.... until then, I will love the plants, and both together. When coming home this afternoon, I was tired, and I found a fine spot under an elm tree, not far from the spot where your *clear sighted folks* had seen me kissing that young girl. I laid down under that tree, and I have learned *half of* the verb *amo! to love.* When I went out at that time I had always my latin grammar in my pocket, so as not to lose any time in resting my legs.

Once in a while we had little squalls about *newspapers.* Whenever there were some bitter articles in the Republican papers about the government, or any thing that indicated that democracy was progressing she would cut it off before she gave it to me. She had a conservative and Royalist paper. So I told her: If you do not give it to me as it comes, I will get a Republican paper. So I did, and that vexed her considerably. I continued to be protestant in my own way.

She did *not believe* I was, but she had to act as if she had, she had to have the appearance, and she *cared* for me and she treated me well, and so her son did, also. Once in a while we had a *row* about my giving meat on Friday to some of her folks who were eating at the same table as I did. One day I had a dish of several squabs (young pigeons) when all the rest, men and women were eating fricasee of *beans* or something of that sort, and cheese, etc. Among them were two young men, working with me in the garden, that would not object to eat some pigeons. I offered them, but they hesitated, but I did not. I said: Do you want any? I took one and cut it in two, and gave each one one-half. They hardly began when the old lady came and saw them. She did not say any thing because she was afraid of a *storm*, but sometime after she came to see me in the greenhouse, and she said: Mr. Gardener, or Louis, she called me so when she was of good humor, and she was so notwithstanding the distribution of pigeons, she said: I do not object you to eat meat on Friday, but I do not want you to give any to my folks. It is enough that I have to pay to the Pope *a dispense* for *my son* and *you!* Well, Madame, I think you might save that money, for I am willing to take the whole responsibility for all of us, and more. Well, that is all right, for you, but I must be responsible—I have my soul to save....do you understand, paying the Pope to eat pigeons?!!....What *sublime* thing *faith* is! Nothing equal, except *stupidity*. I do not know if she has saved her soul. Nobody can know that, but if she did not it was not for lack of credulity, for she would swallow any thing the priests would tell her. I recollect once, a tall, swarthy fellow, just (he said) coming from the Holy Land with *splinters* of the wood of the "Holy Cross," and something *rarer yet:* some bones of *Saint Vincent,* the saint venerated by the "*vine dressers,*" probably because he was a liberal consumer of their produce!? I do not affirm, I only ask the question. He (the discoverer of *traps to catch* the simple-hearted, with an *iron-clad faith,* managed, with the aid of *co-swindlers,* to persuade her to get some and have them *enshrined.* She did so! and I understood that it cost her 2,000 francs ($400), at a time she was so hard up that she could not pay me on my salary $20. I wanted to go to Paris.. to see the philosophers—drinkers of *essence* of beef, but *not eating* the *meat* for fear of losing their souls!! O! stupiditas stupiditarum! O, God!!....have mercy upon them! they deserve....to inherit the kingdom of Heaven and eat hay....

To finish with this *good hearted* woman, and the priest (*of whom, I wish to be plainly understood*, I do not *include the whole of them*, for there are a great number worthy of our *admiration*, whether believers or unbelievers, Jews, Catholics, Protestants, Mahomedan—*charity, philanthropy*, exist everywhere. *Virtues* are cosmopolitan as are *vices*. I do not *hate* men, priests or others, *I hate* the *principles*, the *institutions* that have a tendency to *deprive humanity* of their *common sense, judgment, reason*....) I must tell you something that will astound you: A young "Abbé" "Abbot" not ordained as a priest yet, had received hospitality from that lady, he being sickly and poor, had been prescribed by doctors to live in the country for his health, which was frail indeed, but he had a great deal of energy, was quick in his movements and wonderfully intelligent, impulsive, passionate to excess, but whose senses, judgment, had been *vitiated* by that clerical mode of torturing one's moral and mental faculties, trying to make you believe that bladders are lanterns, gas lamps, etc.... We had a billiard table on the place, but nobody to play with him except the old lady, who could not stand round the billiard table more than a few minutes and she was out of breath, then she send for me. He had never held a cue in his life, but in less than half a day he could handle it as well as I did my spade, but of course he was apt to miss a ball and that made him nervous. He wore a sort of *tea cup* saucer cap that he took off, threw it on the floor and trampled it over and said: Shall I ever be able to play and *beat* you? I replied, not in dancing on your cap. In that very moment I had to leave him. He looked at me with consternation. Will you not come back? I told him I would try, but I did not. I had something to do that prevented me. He was in terrible agitation. Will you play again to-morrow? I may possibly, but I have some thing to do. I can't play all the time. What do you care Mrs..... my priestified lady had told him that I would, that may be but.... no but you must, the lady was just coming and both of them coaxed me so I did play longer than I wished. I did not dislike it, but I did not want to play by the day. When he could make a carombol he was a happy man, but when he missed it he was like the "D.... in a holy water pot." *He had become* so passionately fond of playing that he would have spent the whole day without eating, but always furious when he missed a ball. One day he got so excited that I told him, Monsieur l'Abbé! it is not becoming for a man of your character, a Christian moralizer, to behave as you do, and if you continue I shall have to quit your company. But I *shall not mind it*, if every time you get fits of impatience you will express your mortifications *in Latin*; he could do it as fluently as in French. Well, he said, I will do it, but as a compensation you will teach me how I could beat you! I can not do that. I shall give you a chance to do it, but I can not demonstrate to you technically. I am not expert enough in that line. I have always been very *superficial* in every thing except in raising plants from *cuttings* or *procreating defenders* for my adopted country.... One day he got so exasperated at my success in playing that an idea got into my head, partly for fun, partly to give him a lesson of Christian humility, but mostly to find out if he knew any thing of Voltaire's writings, that *nightmare* of the clerical progeny. He had got in such a passion when missing a carombol, that at once I picked up his cap, handed it to him, and with all the dignity I could assume I recited to him those four verses of *Voltaire* (tragedy of Mahomet):

> "Ne sais tu pas encore, homme faible et superbe,
> "Que l'insecte insensible enseveli sous l'herbe,
> "Et l'aigle impérieux qui plane en haut du ciel
> "Rentrent dans le néant aux yeux de l'éternel!

Knowest thou not yet, man weak and haughty,
That the insensible insect, enshrouded under the sod,
And the imperious eagle that soars to heaven lofty,
Re-enter into chaos in the eyes of God!

When he saw my countenance, heard my scanned declamation, he threw his cue across the billiards, and said: What is that? Who has written those verses — they are admirable! I responded with a studied calmness: *Voltaire!!* No! he said, that *wretch* has never written such sublime expressions. He has, Monsieur l'Abbé! or *I lie*, and you are a two *legged ass!* But you are not an ass, nor *do I lie*, and Voltaire is a *terrestrial* genius. He *saw*. He had *seen* more of God in his cabinet than all your theologians have ever seen in the pulpit, or from the pulpit.... I have faith in your frankness, but I cannot believe that a *miscreant* like him could have had such admiration of God and expressed it in such a noble style. Let us see no more of your expression — *miscreancy*. He had *no faith* in your *nonsenses*, and you, have too much in your theologians, *in absurdo*. If I show you those verses, printed half a century ago, will you believe it? I did not wait for his answer, but I went for the volume containing the verses. He read them, and some few more. Then looked on the title page of the book to see if there were no tricks, put his hand on his forehead, tucked up his hair and involuntarily said:

"*Sacredié!—je n'aurais pas cru.*" — "I would not have believed it." .... Sacredié, on the lips of a Catholic priest, is an *euphemism* for damned, damnation, etc. He looked like a dog that had been flogged. I said no more but young man (I was, perhaps, a few months older than he was), it is time to go to bed. No, he said, we have time enough, and if you do not wish to play any more, let us go in the parlor. We shall talk about plants, of which 1 know absolutely nothing — those cryptogamic minute plants you showèd once on the *trunk* of that *beach* tree, where you quoted that verse of Virgil: (—— " *O Tityre patulœ recubans sub tegmine fagi,*" under the shade of that beech tree, only we were standing up, while Virgil's shepherd was reclining), have interested me much — they have infused in me the desire to know more. We went in the parlor, but we did not talk long about plants, and the conversation soon crept in that rather *hollow science*, theology. It was about 7 *or* 8 P.M. when we went, and when we quitted it was 4 *o'clock*, A.M. That parlor was a room perhaps twenty or twenty-five feet square, with ceilings fourteen feet high, and only a wood fire of logs, eight or ten or more inches in diameter, that roasted us in front, and we were chilled behind. It was in October or November—I am not sure—but it was not warm. The *heat* of our polemics kept us from shivering. It was about 11 *o'clock* when our lady sent her maid to quench the fire, dreading we should quarrel. She knew our temper, and she acted accordingly. However, she was disappointed. We both saw her, the maid, breaking the logs, half burnt, and burying them in the ashes. We were so excited that neither one of us would say a word to stop her — perhaps she would not have paid an attention because she had been ordered to do it, *volens nolens*. So we remained as I have said until 4 *a. m.* When we parted he told me *Mr. Louis,* some other day we shall resume our *conference.* I want to *convince* you! Well if that is your aim you will be deceived. You ought to know it by to-night's experience. You have acknowledged *twice* that you were *touched*, and you did not touch me once. Because you are too *obstinate*. No!! but because your arguments are *too dull.* Your best arguments were the *Holy Scriptures!* Who has written these *apocryphal* books? the logicians of the *Apocalypse?* This is another *authority* which is as *clear* as *a bottle of ink*.... Good night! *Bonne nuit! Au revoir!* We met the following day. I *mean* at 7 or 8 o'clock in the morning of that day. The following day he had to rejoin his regiment in his *barrack seminary* at *Reims,* where I saw him once more in the "*grand seminary,*" where he was Professor of Theology. We began an argument but on such a high diapason that he suddenly told me we *must part.* Here the *walls have ears!* So we shook hands and he ran away saying Adieu! adieu! in aeternum! I repeated the phrase, and ... After I reached here (America) I wrote to him *once*. He answered me, but he had *misunderstood* me in *some remarks* I had made the first Sunday I was in New York, about the *multitude* of religious *creeds* and what I had seen in three different churches I had visited, that he had concluded that I gave the *prominence* to the Cath.... His answer was such, that I felt so indignant, I never wrote him again, his *ultramontanism* had broken all the ties of sympathy between us. I suppose he had understood when I was in France that my *Protestantism* was only *platonic*. It was and it was *not*. I am according to my notions a *Protestant* as ever. I *protest* against what does not agree with my ideas, my conscience, but I do it silently. I try not to hurt any body's feelings. I let every one do as they please, and I wish to enjoy the same privilege. *Even* in my own family, where I ought to have something to say, I let every one of my children do as they please in *spiritual affairs*. I have tried, I try yet to inculcate in them some principles of good behavior, honesty, tolerance, friendly relations with every one *worthy* of having their associations *cultivated!* Only one thing I *shall never tolerate:* " *Auricular confession*," *for me* one of the greatest *social evils* at *least* for the 30 first years of my life. Now I hear nothing of it.

Again, I want to be *understood* that *I do not* think that any one going to confess is *wrong*, not at all. I *firmly* believe that there are immense quantities of people professing that creed that are *sincere*, but the *exceptions* do not alter the rule.... I do not know how long I have to vegetate on this globe, but as long as I do I shall — it will be as it has been since I have been able to think for myself. Respecting the religious and political opinions of every one whoever they may be, every one of us is responsible for one's deeds before the *Eternal!*............

ELUCIDATION SOLICITED.

A lady amateur—scrutinizer of *genesis affairs*, has asked me if I would be willing to give the initial particulars of my first sight of that " Phanerogyne," in Astoria, in 1840. I have replied in the affirmative that I would do it with a vivid pleasure, for it will give me a regain of those *celestial sensations* I have experienced in that providential circumstance. Even to-day, the mere souvenir of it makes me feel as if my heart was melting in a sea of voluptuousness!

The first glimpse I had of that cryptogamous specimen of vegetation, was through (rather a dim light) the front sashes of a greenhouse. *She*, as now, I know the sex which I did not then, whether it was diœcious, hermaphrodite, or unisexual. She was walking in the carriage road of the site we were on, looking on each side, in the borders, to see the flowers. She *seemed* to be afraid—of what I could not tell; I found it after. It was that "Albany *Dutchman*" that had been depicted to her as a good intelligent fellow enough, but, an awful radical or red republican who would kill *his man!* as he would a fly, etc., etc. — any qualification of that sort.

My second look at her, always through the glazed sashes, brought to my mind that rule of Latin and French grammar: "Gallus escam quærens, margaritam reperit," anglicé, "A cock searching for food, found a pearl!" That which I translated off-hand in my mind, "Gallina, a hen, searching for flowers, found" — an admirer, a lover, or a husband! You see that I *did not lack* presumption. I confess it now, but I would not have done it then, though, shortly after, two or three days later, when we came in contact, I felt the same sensation, *ambition* to possess her, but I did not express it; although I have always been somewhat apt to blunder I did not in that instance. I kept my *dignity* though, according to the *friendly reports* at that time, I could or would *kill a man*, but at the same time I would not have slighted a woman. In that first encounter, we had very nearly *collided*. She was turning round a building to see me, and I was coming in the opposite direction, walking fast, when we almost fell in each other's arms, or at least *face* to *face*. Was not that a strange coincidence? We both looked at each other, as you may fancy, *with surprise!* for neither of us were prepared to such a sudden encounter. In a few seconds we had recovered our wits. Then she told me: Mr. Louis, (that was my appellation there) I wanted to see you, to ask you if you would sell me a flower stem of tuberose .... I shall not tell you what I answered........ You may say whatever you please. I have written the *dots*, you may write the *Is*, just to suit you. You may *guess*, as I do when I am in doubt. But I am willing to tell you that: We had a long conversation in French. My English would not have been adequate to express all I had *not on* hand, but in my heart. I suppose you might wish to know what we said to each other. I wish I could, but it is impossible for me to tell you now, nor immediately after, except we talked, perhaps, over an hour, and we might have talked three or four, or more, but she was called and warned that if she should delay any longer she would miss the boat coming from Flushing, to go to New York, then to Albany. I did not know where to; it is after, I found it. On reflection, I think we talked on American, English, French morals theatrical performances, practical theology, *Tuberosology*, and many other topics profane and religious, in logy or logies, etc. All I recollect perfectly well is that we understood each other almost by *intuition*. The sequel has proved it, for *half a century*, and *two months strictly* speaking, though *two weeks* less in *reality*. " Man proposes! God disposes!" .... Human kind progress more or less successfully. The laws of Nature remain as God created them — *unchangeable*, notwithstanding what may be our desires—our wishes to have rain when too dry, or dry when too wet....

Let me remember, if I have not omitted some details in my narrative of our henceforth discovery of that individuality now belonging to the community as far as the name is concerned, as to the possession, *Nihil!* The thing discovered remains to the *Finder!*

O! I remember now, the *dread* of that Mr. Louis came from the folks who gave the "*dearly* paid for hospitality" to Miss Jackson and her Albany friends. It seems that after meals, and from taking sea baths, the conversation ran on *that demagogue!* I have never been and never will, but even if I had been I deserved some regards from those people who were continually begging of me a loaf of bread, butter, etc., when *short*, and that was the rule, short of bread and butter, and shorter of decency, and those loaves were *never* returned. The head of that family was an ex—of some sort of French Nobility. He styled himself—I forget — but his name was a sort of Latin "Servatius," that my employer, Mr. George Thorburn, called "Starvation!" — a well applied name, for often he lived on *Lobsters* he caught in the Hell Gate waters, and the loaves of bread and oil and vinegar he extorted from my housekeeper, who, she told me, had not the will to refuse his poor wife and children, half *starved*; hence the appellation.... "Starvation!!" Not being able or willing to reciprocate our compassion he thought that some calumnies, well contrived, would answer to represent me as a hero of abjections in the eyes of his boarders, who had temporarily broken *his forced vigils*, for as long as they were with him he had enough to eat, and after meals to help his digestion and make my panegyric he told them, that Mr. Louis was a d.... of a fellow when talking politics, that "The Declaration of the Rights of Man" was my *bible*, that I thought a man like me was equal to any nobleman, according to merits, and such utopias. That when I left France I had a *wife* and several children. I wondered he did not attribute me as many as the *wise King Solomon* had; it is true that he could not very well do that — the antithesis would have been too *metaphorical* from a king to a demagogue, and especially to make it swallow, to a professor of French at the Military Academy of West Point, with whom I had had a long conversation a few days before, who, I understood after, told that apologist of my virtues, that from our conversation he had had no inductions that I was such a *diabolical* man as he depicted me, but quite the contrary, and asked him who had given him such information, unless I had myself, and that was not very likely. Later he told me that he had no idea that man was so contemptible, that he belonged to a good family, etc. However, all those calumnies did not hurt me, on the contrary, their exaggeration confirmed these people, and Miss Jackson, my future wife, that all those reports were to hurt me, out of spite because I would not associate with them, for some motives that I cannot explain here in a decent manner. The conclusion of all that was I got rid of their importunities, and shortly after they had to leave the place, not being able to pay their rent.

I suppose that the lady who has solicited the initial of the particulars of my prowesses — doings in that eccentric love affair has been satisfied, that I have mentioned faithfully the whole incidents? I have, so far, as the departure from Astoria of Miss Jackson, and her friends, Mr. and Mrs. Molinard of Albany goes, but no farther.

The whole and the most important object at stake: The fowling of the bird, was only in its incipiency. I had only seen the colors of her feathers and the outlines of the extremities of her wings, at rest, not flying. Considerable time elapsed before I could have her *caged*. I had to use some substitute for bird's lime to daub her wings to keep her from flying off, though I had not the slightest idea she would do it. Yet in one instance, *unaware, unconscious,* she made an *attempt* to know what sort of a bird catcher I was, in writing me a letter, so *untimely*, so *indiscreetly*, that I almost gave up the chase, the bird, the cage and all, and more. ....Had any body seen me then, when I got the intimation of that *irruption* would have thought I was to give up the soul. It was, as if one had taken my heart — with a pair of nippers to pull my heart out of my body....However, I did not give up any thing at all, but notwithstanding my *love* — some one will say that I was not in love, or else I would not have spoken as I did — I *was in love*, I *have been*, and I am yet, *retrospectively* and *permanently* as long as *I live*, yet at that moment, I clung to my *dignity*, my love *despised*, call it what you please....N. B.—I was in Astoria, and she was at Albany. Had we been both present that would have been only a *lovers' quarrel*, which is a condiment to flavor the thing!!....I wrote a letter— two letters. I have them yet, with her answers, also, in which I *fulminated*, *exhausted* all the choicest flowers of my rhetoric, to convince her, and I *did convince her* deeply, so deeply that she answered me at once, to come to Albany, that we could never understand each other by correspondence, that she could not tell what she felt, by *writing*, but she would make *verbally*, a confession that would *deserve* my absolution *without* the confession, but that she expected a reciprocity of generosity for her *venial sin*....

Two weeks later than the above incident we were, as I *now* fancy, were Adam and Eve, after the lunch of the forbidden apple, drinking the sweet sap of the ....I do not know what to say to make an adequate comparison. I leave it to any of those who have been in similar circumstances as I was, after all my tribulations, metamorphosed into "Byron's" *intoxication* — not from intoxication of liquors, but by the capillary attractions of two souls....

Now, you know all that I can tell you without violating the sacred laws of intimacy.

Your Birds-catcher, with only a stem flower of Tuberose and a little perseverance and *cum dignitate*, and reciprocal esteem.

> "Judges and senates have been bought for gold,
> Esteem and love were never to be sold." — POPE.

L. MENAND.

1874, BOSTON, MASS., HORTICULTURAL EXHIBITION.

In my exposition of facts connected with horticulture I have forgotten some, of which I have been remembered accidentally by coming across some *medals* awarded to me by the Massachusetts Horticultural Society.

In 1874, for instance: a *silver medal* for a collection of *Agaræ!* for which to-day, the same society would not probably allow *one* to exhibit, but would rather, if compelled to do it, offer a *gold one* to keep the collection *at home.*

Why ? I cannot very well explain that *eccentric idea*, except by some round-about way, circumlocutory comparisons, *e. g.*, why are the *camellias* since a few years *ostracized ? ?* Is it because they might engender Microbs ? or because they are not ornamental euough, or too common, like the *Crotons ?* Or likely for some other futile unavowable reason, that *some* know but will not divulge, because the confession would not be very creditable.........

Appendix.

In the same year as quoted above, 1874, a specimen of Croton Wiesemanni, or to be up to the progress of botanical science, Codiæum Wiesmannianum or only C. Wiesmanni, if the *anum* termination is found too long, however, the two adjectives are contestable *grammatically* speaking. I mean *Wiesmanni* or *ii* and *ianum*. I was going to say that in 1874, the first prize for the best variegated or foliaged plant was awarded to *C. Wiesmann*........and it *deserved* it.

It was a splendid plant, but not handsomer than to-day, only it was younger, terrible thing to be old, I know something of it.

And what can be said to-day about Camellias? In 1844 or 45, two plants of one variety, I think, *C. Mrs. P. Wilder*, came from Boston, hither to Albany, with a bill of $24 for the pair! of *Microbs !* No ! but *Greeks* for all that, *microscopic*, they had a couple of leaves, each with 2 eyes—buds that promised to start in *the future*. I was offered one by the owner of them for half the price paid $12. I declined, because my means did not afford to buy them, yet they were not handsomer than to-day. Notwithstanding the whimsicalities of the day they are handsomer than one-third, if not more so, of all the plants cultivated to-day, including the Orchidaceous plants. Old *Fogyism 1 hear*, I admit that epithet, when it questions a large number of plants whose only merit was to be *rare* and *costly*, but not Camellias or many of the Crotons (not all), and great many other plants, such as: Medinella Magnifica, Rogiera, Toxicophlæa, Thunbergiana, Daphne, Indica rubra, Araucaria pubescens, etc., etc. I beg your pardon. I forgot that I am preaching in the desert.... You have ears but you do not want to hear, so I will close on that subject, and conclude what I have to say on that exhibition. I had also a Phalænopsis, grandiflora var. aurea in bloom on the 17th of September, rather *early*, I understood at that time that it was the first one seen in Boston. I got a medal for it and $25. I had more plants on exhibition, besides those mentioned, but I could not compete. The rules and regulations did not allow any one out of Massachusetts to do so.

From that year they altered their by-laws, etc., and it was open to *all*. I never went again since, it was too expensive for my means. However, I take great pleasure here, to acknowledge that the whole Society from the President, Mr. Marshal T. Wilder (I think, but I am not sure), to the last members I received the most fraternal attention I have ever received anywhere.

Let God bless you *all.* I in imagination and across

the space that separates us shake your hand with all the effusions of my heart.

The young Anthophilus of nearly forty years ago — of old time, now an old man, a *geron* a *senex*, but always cordially yours,

L. MENAND.

"CONFESSIONS," "GARDENEROLOGY" AND "MISCELLANEOUS."

Please, let me draw my breath for a few minutes, then I shall continue my narration..........

Now, behold! my friends : I begin to believe that I have recounted enough of my recollections, and that it is high time I should come to the peroration of my long spinning digressions, more or less edifying, but rather the latter, and close the sluice of my overflowing loquacity on that subject, and by resuming what I have told you of my life as a man and as a gardener, etc., etc.

Have you ever been impressed with the idea that the profession of a gardener is somewhat *extraneous* in the existence of a man? Of a gardener! Yes, of a *gardener!!* That interjection seems to surprise you, for I fancy from your hypothetical silence, that if you had anything to say, you would say this : What the d—— does he mean with such question? Well, I mean (as I have no false modesty, and do not wish to be as reticent as you are), that a gardener who has the *will* — the *determination* — can be a very important item in the community at large.

From the beginning of the world up to this day, they have acted in the comedy of human life very important parts. First and foremost, I must proceed by gradations, and be careful not to say anything that would *exalt* too much your *pride*, as gardeners, as well as the rest of mankind, are not exempt of vanity in the *occasion*. I want to convince you, as I am *convinced* myself, of the importance of our profession. Who was the first gardener, before our grandmother Eve was born? Adam, is it not? Well, *who* cultivated the first garden? The Eden garden — not the Eden garden of New York city, but the *true, genuine,* "*Eden Garden*" of old time! I now forget in what part of the globe it was, exactly; but I think it was not in our Western hemisphere; but you know what I mean.........

Who planted and cultivated the first apple trees? God! you will say. I admit that, of course; but who took care of the orchard? Always Adam! And without any attendant; he had no foreman; he was alone; he had no boss but God, and God had given him "carte-blanche;" he could do what he pleased; besides I understand that God did for him, *when needed,* what he has done for me, *six thousand or more* years after. He, Adam, had to work hard to keep every thing in good condition; and at that time there were no ploughs, no agricultural implements of any kinds, as to-day. I am not sure, even, if he had a spade, and a scythe to mow the lawns. Sometimes he fell asleep on the grass, and it was during one of those naps that *God* pulled one of his ribs to make our mother, Eve, in order that he should have an helpmate, to assist him in his *light* agricultural and horticultural operations; such as picking up fallen fruit among the grass, and after a more intimate acquaintance to become his "*Phanerogyne,*" and then to study cryptogamy — pshaw! I meant to say "progeny!" for I do not believe there were any cryptogamous plants then; even the science of progeny was not known; and this last science must have been known and well understood before any one could study the first *cryptogamy*....and a useless one, almost, and an *aristocratic science*. While "*progeny*" is the science "par excellence," even *superior* to *arithmetic*, for *one* must be expert in the former before he can study the latter; for without that "*divine science,*" "progeny," that "sine qua non," without which nothing can be had, *here*, I feel the *itching* of scribendi, loquendi et cognoscendi, *to write, to talk,* and to *know, especially*, what was the variety of the apple cultivated on the grounds of Paradise. I would be willing to give something to know it. The reason I speak of that here, is, that I have asked a professor of theology, said to be well posted in "Genesis" affairs, and he told me he knew nothing about, but suggested, with an appearance of sound logic, that our fraternity, gardeners, pomologists, and other "sui generis" of that description, ought to be more apt to elucidate that enigma than theologians, who only concern themselves with God's direct affairs, and not with such accessory trifles as knowing the names of what he grew in his country seat. I really feel much disappointed, for I expected to be able to get the right name of that apple, or *orange*, that tempted our first mother, and communicate it to you. Some one has hinted to me that that apple might have been an orange, but I do not believe it. I know there was, in old time, a celebrated garden called the "Garden of Hesperides," where the *apples were oranges !* That substitution of one name for another might have answered for the *Olympic Gods*, but it will not do for us practical profanes and rather sceptical although *we have* in our *mottled* fraternity some fellows that are apt to try to make us *swallow pills* of *aloes* and *rhubarb*, for aperitive lozenges, and they often succeed, but you may be *assured* that it is not for those *tricksters* that I am puzzling my mind to let them know the name of the Eden's apple. They might try to change its name and sell it to some *inno-*

cent for an *evergreen, ever-bearing* golden pumpkin, and they would find customers ! !

Gardeners have also acted remarkably well in the city of Babylon under the reign of the Queen Semiramis, to lay out the famous suspended gardens of that city, where stood the celebrated Tower of Babel, whence came the confusion of languages. I have never heard of the peach, and apricot, plum trees, etc., etc., trained as espaliers on the surface of those immense walls, 60 *miles* in circumference, 87 *feet* thick, and 350 *high !* If the gardeners of that time have grown trees to cover those walls on the whole surface, I must *congratulate* them, and own that they have *distanced* our modern gardeners by as many *miles* ahead as their walls were higher than ours only I should like to know *how high* were the *ladders* they used to train the trees? I fancy I hear some fellows say : Mr. Menand ! we like jokes, but you carry them too far. Now, my friends ! I wish you to understand me, I have not measured those walls, as you, I do not believe they were so high. But I have copied those descriptions from what you name " Holy Scriptures " ! ! ! If you do not believe in them I can not help it, that is your business. Only I will pass the remarks, that if you disbelieve " Holy Writs " you will compromise your salvation ? This incredulity of yours annoys me, because I have not got through my narration on the subject I am writing, and if you do not believe it is useless for me to waste so much paper, at all events I will finish to scribble this page. Noah, also, *somewhat* belonged to our fraternity, however, he was more a *specialist*, he grew grape vines, as many of you only grow roses or carnations, every one has his hobbies. His hobby was what to-day we call *œnophilist*, in plain English, a grape grower, not *table grapes*, but varieties of grapes to make wine *oinos*. He was a good old man, but some of his contemporaries, likely jealous of his successes in grape culture, said he was still more fond of the juice of the grape, than of the cultivation of it, and besides that he had another hobby, more *scientific*, but no better if not studied with moderation and judgment. He studied the laws of "*gravitation*," and with such zeal that often he was found lying on the ground, trying to take his *centre of gravity*. I do not know if he ever wrote anything about that *science gravitation*. All I know is that he taught our ancestors to cultivate the grape, and that alone deserves his name to go to posterity, and the gratitude of all those thousands of people who grow the grape on a large scale.

But where gardeners have been famous it is from the decline, the fall of the Roman empire. During the dark days, the middle ages, until the French Revolution in 1792, then they became *eminent*, as gardeners in the convents, *especially* convents of the feminine sex, where no men were *admitted*, but some of that craft. Is not that creditable to us? We must be *endowed* of some virtue we are not aware of. I know we are somewhat expert in the way of *vegetable procreation*, and, also, a little in the animal procreation, but, in what, some of us, excel, it is in the procreation of plants *nomenclature*. I wish I should know them. I would, with pleasure, write their panegyric in glowing expressions. I can not quote anything particular of the prowesses of any of our friends in those convents, but I have read a great many stories and even "*histories*" of their capacities in many ways, but you would not believe me — you would think I am joking, consequently I shall not say anything. But, another incident in which I am concerned, and which I hope you will accept as true. It is a reminiscence of what you have partly read before. That Lady, for whom I have been gardener over six years. She had been in a convent until she got 16 or 17 years old. Then her parents entrusted her to a professor of procreation (a husband) who completed her education. She did not give me any information about the gardeners in that place, except that they grew excellent Green-Gage plums — " Reine Claude," the queen of *all* the plums, by *name* and *quality*, and that it was there she learned to *preserve* them in *Brandy*, candied *with sugar!* the *souvenir* alone of those plums makes "my mouth water." I have never since "*eating-drinking*" such *delicious* thing. "*A Daisy*," would say a certain Scotchman friend of mine. I say "*Celestial!*" In 1878, when in Paris, my wife, and one of my daughters, searched all the most *renowned* confectionery stores to find them, and *failed,* and I, on my own side, did the same, with the same success — failed. Is not this long digression a *sin?* but a *venial one,* and I confess it. Now that WE have eaten — and drunk the plums, in imagination, let us return to my Lady, and her maid, both ex-*nuns*. At the advent of the first empire of Napoleon, the 1st, they had lived in Paris, frequenting the court, and when came the *downfall* of that same empire in 1815, they came in that convent or monastery, where I was monk and gardener. I cumulated the professions, but I had only a *salary* for *one*, and for my monkish, or monachism, I had *plums in Brandy*. I had some, also, as a gardener. I had the control of them while on the trees. O! I forgot that same blessed Lady and her maid treated me well. I tell you all those *little nothings*, to corroborate what I have said about gardeners as an exception from other profession. Those two nuns of that worldly nunnery, practiced hospitality to that extent, that one day after

I had parted from some gardeners-visitors—they came to me and told me: Louis, why do you not treat your visitors with more cordiality? It was the custom then in the country, at that time, to offer dinner to any one (in my category) who came, and always some distance from their homes. You treat them very unceremoniously; you always give them ordinary wine; why do you not give them some sparkling champagne? I do not for many reasons. Firstly, I do not particularly care for most of them, who, in the occasion, would call me heretic, *blood drinker*, etc. As for the other ones, if I should do it, they would tell the other ones — the *cold-shouldered*, who would call me an *aristocrat*, with accessory epithets, so in order *not* to deviate from my principles of *equality* I treated them all alike: "Equality before *my law*." Not the government's laws that deny me the right of voting because I paid no taxes, etc., and I *work* for a *salary!* Does anybody work for or without no salary? Yes, I did *work* for salary, but many get *salary* and do *not* work at all!! How do you call that law?....I understood at that time, that the *best* country in the *world* for *high salary* and often *nothing to do* was *old England*, but I suppose there are good many other nations where they have such workers—where there is nothing to do, and good pay!! However, I did not care much for any of them, *not* that I had any dislike for them, but their ideas, their principles or manners did not sympathize with mine. I liked solitude, and they did not. When alone I could soliloquize, even dialogize. I put a question, a dilemma, and I solved them myself, without a judge. Was it not like in a convent? But it was about the same. Only the few *nuns* were old—60, 65, and perhaps more, and young ones were out of reach, so I was almost a saint, although I heard some one, in speaking of me, say: that I was a d...., with a meliorating adjective, such as *a fellow* good or bad, but such an epithet does not disturb the equanimity of young philosophers, for I already began to philosophize, for just at that time my Lady, my employer, asked me one day: "Mr....., The gardener, or Mr. Louis," I forget. Why, when you write to my son, why do you not address your letters "Monsieur Le Baron! De Mont," — Mr. the Baron of Montgenet? Because I do not know what a *Baron* is, Madam! You know very well what it is, but your *silly* notions of Democracy forbid you from calling him by his *title*. Is it not so? Well, Madame! I confess it is so. I know what it means *for me*—it means *zero*—*nothing*, and I think it is *more silly* than my *Democracy*, which means "power of the people." I know all these empty words, such as Baron, Duke, and so forth, but you, *Madame!* you do not know that the "Convention Nationale"—that *memorable*, that *grandest* political *assembly* that *ever existed*, that did not play *ducks and drakes* with flat stones, *have abolished* all the *titles! ! !* without any exceptions. But, *I add*, that if *it* or *they* had not done it, I would do it on my *own* authority and *responsibility* without paying any dispense to the Pope! When I write to your son, I address my letters as the French politeness requires it—" Monsieur Montgenet." He has never complained of it, but if he does, I am very sorry, but I cannot help it. I must abide to the laws, although I have little respect for many of them.

My friends! from what I have told you of my behavior in that *convent* I have been thinking, on reflexions, that you *might* be impressed with the idea (and I am slightly afraid of it) that my doings there were not very exemplary, if I have not exaggerated one way or the other. I have *not;* all I have told, recounted to you, has been to the *letter* except in writing. I have selected my expressions but I *did not* change the meaning of the facts or circumstances in any way or manner. If I had *always* acted as I have told you, notwithstanding they cared for me, I could not have remained there over six years. The life of humanity is somewhat like the atmosphere we live in, changeable. For a certain lapse of time we have fine, bright weather, then suddenly we get cloudy, stormy, rough weather, then fair again. So it was with me, but as a rule the atmosphere was SERENE! and if you should analyze all I have related, you will be convinced it must have been so.

I made up in devotion, zeal, attention, *not solicited*, what I was deficient in temperament. I cannot tell the particulars of many incidents, it would be too tedious even for me, and much more so for those who may read them. Only one instance out of many. We had many thousand square yards of soil to remove two or three hundred yards off to build a greenhouse, and all that in wheelbarrows. No horses could be employed, it had to be done by bipeds. It was the heaviest job I have ever had on my hands. I had four or five, sometimes six men, each one with a wheelbarrow, and I filled them up as quick as they could carry them. When we began the son of my Lady employer, told me and those men, with me, too, that I could not continue steady. It was getting late in the season and I was very anxious the work should be done, so that it stimulated my courage, and to stimulate more efficaciously the energy of my co-bipeds our old Lady sent us, on the spot we were working, a large jug of wine, with bread and cheese, for the men to eat and drink, *ad libitum* between their meals of course, when eating and drinking. They had to rest of course. It amused me wonderfully to see the way they twisted a piece of bread and cheese and swallowing the claret. Those men were feasting, and I, looking at them, so that we were all enjoying, every one his own way, the *son* of our prioress of the convent asked me several times "why don't you eat and drink like those men, you work as much as they do and more." That may be so, but those men do not eat as much *good solid food* in two or three days as we do in one meal. What those men *drink especially* and stimulated them would have had the contrary effect with me, " *the drinking* especially." I have always talked a great deal and probably oftener more than necessary, but *never* under the influence of liquor. I have always been in DREAD to hear any one speaking of me and saying *of me* as I have often times heard people speaking of men under the influence of liquor say "That man is *drunk*." It is not *him* who speaks, but the liquor, he is drunk. I am not *very sure* if 1 have not made the *above* remark about *drinking* to warn you that all I have said from the beginning of my prolix narrations of my recollections, digressions and the rest is to let you understand that *all* I have said comes from *the heart*, not from of *a bottle*, unless the bottle of *ink*.

So that I will come to the conclusion that, as I have told you has been, partly to indulge my notions, to let

off the surplus of steam that would condense in my
head; this last is a hygienic prescription with me; and
to try to convince you, as I am convinced myself, that
gardeners have many chances to improve their material
and intellectual conditions; more than many of other
professions, if they are a little willing to observe the
circumstances in which they are, and use their tact and
judgment, and not go forward too quick, according to
my observations. In that said convent, where I had
been cloistered over six years, I have *almost* always
acted diametrically opposed to everybody else. I was
surrounded with bigotry, hypocrisy, superstitions, ignorance, jealousies, etc. I have criticised, laughed,
sneered at many of their religious performances, *would-
be* morality, etc. I suppose that often I have hurt
the feelings of many, and yet after a while, on reflex-
ion, they have always acknowledged to me that I was
right. Even since I have come in contact with people
of all classes of society in my business, I have had some
difficulties with some of them, *even rupture*, but after
a few months or years, they have all come and told me
that *We!* had been wrong. I have always said that
I had been sorry, but in the same circumstances I would
do it again. They *included* me in the *We*, but I did
not admit the *association*. I have followed my *own
lines*, like Gen. Grant did, only I have not reaped as
many *Laurels* (*Laurus nobilis, sweet bay*), as he did,

and the few I have left nobody wants them to-day. I have *to deck* myself with, or use the leaves as a condiment to flavor " Beef à-la-mode," or other dishes; that which is rather *unglorious* but is *palatable* if not as *glorious as a sword scar* across the face. One can't have everything....be a Hero and have good dishes though both might be.... Now, my friends and co-laborers, let us —— (if you feel toward me as I do toward you), shake hands, for it is probably the last opportunity we shall have to do it, at least on this sublunary planet; as to the one above, I have only hope........

      Cordially yours,
       L. MENAND.

P. S. Allow me, before we part, to salute you with the French formula of the Revolution of 1792, just a century *this year:*

"Liberty, Equality, Fraternity, Forever—for—Eternity!"

        ANTHOPHILUS,
    Of nearly forty years ago, *alias*
      L. MENAND, in 1892.

THE HAUNTED HOUSE.

Candidly, I thought I had recounted every incident of my life worth relating. When yesterday returning from Albany, in the electric car, and in passing opposite the original spot of my *debuts as a florist*, etc. — the, now, Aged Men philanthropic Asylum, on the Albany and Troy road, I was suddenly and forcibly reminded of the *legendary* reputation of that building as being a "Refuge" of the spooks, ghosts, and hobgoblins of the town of Watervliet, in 1842, and probably long before. We had hired the place for five years. We hardly were moved in than some of the few and far apart neighbors informed me that they were surprised that I had hired the place for such a long lease, that nobody could live in it but a short time, on account of the aforesaid progenies of the devil, rather week minds, or something equal to it. The speaker of the assembly of those informants told with a wonderfully emphatic gesture that he would not *sleep* in it one *single night*, if he was offered *a* 1,000 *dollars!!* Was not such a disclosure an appaling calamity: in the *United States of North America*, in the middle of the Nineteenth Century? Hallucinations of some poor-minded ignorant people, some persons will say in justification of the community at large. Alas! it was not so, being obliged to live there five years I had occasion to be convinced myself that the credulity was not confined in a few poor country people uneducated, but spread in all classes of society.

We had been living in that ghost's refuge for eighteen or twenty months, I cannot exactly tell. We had two persons living with us, a servant girl, and a man working with me. My wife was almost every day in the week in Albany from 8 A. M. to 4 P. M. About that time we lost our second child, the first having died in Astoria, a few months later we had a daughter, the oldest one of seven boys and girls, six living with me or near me now, 1892 — we had to get a nurse, a large, stout, immense woman, whom from the appearance one could have supposed she could nurse up half a dozen, still the child did not thrive well. She slept in the same room with my wife on a cot bed at the foot of my wife's bed. One morning early I went in the room to see how they were all, mother, child and nurse, when in a great excitement — a flurry — said that she would not sleep in that house another night, for any thing in the world, that the greatest part of the night she had been *tossed* or rather *heaved* up as if by the swelling of waves under the cot-bed, not a very disagreeable sensation I should think, but frightful for her, understand: that, that woman must have weighed 225 or 250, so you may imagine what a strong *ghost* or *devil* it must have been to lift her, from that time she never came any more in the house but in day time, but she never neglected to divulge the incident of having been *tossed* by spooks and everybody believed the story as she did herself, and every one wondered how it was that neither of us *four* in the house did not hear any thing, but I heard from my young man, who saw all the folks round us, that we were French folks who did not care for the spooks or the devil and perhaps we had some fellow-feelings — sympathy for them, or else they would not have spared us any more than our *mammoth Venus*. That monumental nurse and her family at that time had to move back in the country near the Shaker Village of Watervliet, whither we had to send our child, her mother not believing in the possibility of nursing a child without the breast of a woman. I object strongly, in one sense, *not that*, the breast was not the most natural in principle, but that the constitution of such a nature, a mass of *inflated flesh* was *uncongenial* to the nutrition of a weak, a delicate child *materially* speaking, and then probably *worse mentally* speaking, nursed up by a *mind haunted* by the existence of *ghosts*, of *spooks impalpable, intangible* things *infusing* her blood in the system of a frail being, it was unnatural, monstrous! In a few weeks the child was dwindling to nothing, when my wife began to be impressed with my idea and said: we must bring her home, but did not think she would ever get any better, that the *nursing bottle* would not be any better, but in a few days the progress of the child regaining her health was so manifest that she got *almost* convinced, not quite, that was natural.... Subsequently in the course of multiplication.... she tried again *herself*.. but in vain.... and hereafter *all* the children we have had were raised by the artificial breast and all have done well, never been sick except as ordinary children illnesses.— Now that my hobgoblin digressions are over, let us return to those believing in the existence of such vagaries. During the four years we remained amongst those harmless imaginary beings we had the visits of three or four parties from Albany and Troy, two especially I remember well, one a gentleman from Albany whose name was Mr. Mitchel or such name. I think he kept the Congress Hotel where the Capitol is now. The place was advertised for sale and he had an idea to buy it. After a few words of introduction he asked me about the location, the quality of the land, etc., to all these informations I answered categorically, minutely to satisfy him, but I perceived by his manner, his countenance, that there was something else, he hesitated to mention.... looking at him I began to think about the ghosts, but I could not believe that such a fine looking man, with such an intelligent appearance could give credence to such silly stories; but always with hesitation he asked if the place was healthy? if the *house* was *quiet?* if no *trouble* in it? etc.—, then I began to look at him seriously and asked him if he was serious in those declamations, *ultra-sensible*, not to use any other more appropriate expressions, I went on— I told him the place was healthy, at least we had never been sick, that the house was *a solid one*, well built on solid slate rock, and no trouble anywhere except in the *vacuum* in our pockets and *a well without water*, but any quantity of toads.... Well he replied, that's not what I want, I want, then he got a litte more explicit.... Many folks say that your *wife* has *lost* her *health*, etc...... *too silly* to be written here.

Only "the phrase": *My wife having lost her health!* I could not very well digest it without bursting with laughing, that which I did with all my heart. Then I told him in good humour and with a good deal of *compassion*. Is it possible, sir! that an intelligent man as you seem to be should believe in such stupidities .... my-wife-having-lost-her-health-through-the-medium-of ghosts, or the devil!!! Well, sir! she has never kept her bed *one second*, except, when she *brought forth* young defenders to our common country, and that *I do not believe was* or *had been caused* by the *interference* of any diabolical agencies....unless ....I....O! God — have pity for us!

This first visitor went away in a very bad humor, partially, because he really wanted the place and that my railleries had not convinced him but half, if any at all. One thing certain he did not buy it, and ultimately I was punished by the proprietor blaming me for having spread the report of the place being *holy-ghosted* in order to prevent him selling it. If you have read the story understandingly you may judge! Yet later I had to pay a *forced* fine for it, you shall see. Shortly after the visit of that innocent man, another came from Troy, equally a wide-awake one, judging from the appearance, but he did not listen to my jestings as patiently as the former, and he abruptly made his exit, from a few words he was grumbling as he walked away, I supposed he did not like my sarcasms, but I think he had as much faith as the former, and both must have come to the conclusion that my incredulity was interested, that I did not want the house should be sold, for if it had according to my agreement I would have had to give up the house and garden, with some compensations, etc. But the fun of it we wished all the time to be out of it, not on account of boarding the spooks gratis; but we were tired of the prospect before us of slow starvation. I must abridge my narrative and tell you how I was punished for my trifling with hobgoblins and for the credulity of those believing in them. The *whole* farm, 18 or 20 or more acres of land, barn and dwelling-house, were valued $500 rent a year, or the house and two acres of garden $300, with the taxes for what I occupied, this last part of the farm; afterward the proprietor would not allow me any thing, saying that the whole taxes were on the *house and garden;* that sort of argumentation did not suit me, and I said that the valuation of the whole concern, farm and garden, was $500, and that I occupied for $300. I would pay accordingly in that proportion, *three-fifths*, and he *two*. He would not hear it, and stuck to his former intention. Finally our lease expired, 1st March, 1847, and we moved where we are now. A short time after we left his place, he married his daughter to a Trojan, who came to live in the house when we hardly had moved our relics. That man was not a proselyte of ghosts, for he came to see me to buy some shrubs, and we had a talk about the spirits. "Well," he said, "I will fix them *all right;* if any, they must be in the *crevices* of the old walls, and I will paper them all over (he was a hang-ing-paper dealer) and fumigate the whole building from cellar to garret." The fact is, that from that time we never heard any thing about the house being disturbed. That sensible man's reason settled the whole, except my litigation with my ex-landlord, who had given me an order for some flowers, I think for the wedding of his daughter with my successor; but since that time he never came to me after, for the settlement of my arrears of rent. I had sent him a bill for them, but he said he would never pay me one cent, for besides the money I owed him and not paid, I had wronged him a great deal for spreading all over that his house was *haunted*. You know ? — what had happened! So you see I was punished for having laughed at people's credulity. However, the difference between us was not much. So ended our intercourse. He has gone to heaven, since many years. I may see him there — if I go, which is ?

L. M.

SKETCH OF A MODERN DISCIPLE OF LOYOLA (BORN IN 1491).

It has been, it seems my destiny ($ANAΓKH'$)* as Victor Hugo has it, that from my cradle to my grave I have been predestined more or less to come in contact with some disciples of my *inspirer* — of these sketches: "St. Ignatius of Loyola," the founder of the "Jesuits Order," *canonized* by the Pope Gregory the *XV.*, and later *suppressed* by the Pope Clement the XIV. in 1773, still "*floruit*" in 1892!!

Bad institutions are as noxious weeds hard to destroy. In consequence thereof, we must do the best we can, if we cannot totally eradicate the evil, to keep off from it, that which in my particular case, is what I have not always done, to my bitter shame, and I humbly confess it, and beg absolution for it — rather late! *true*, but to excuse me if I fall back on the English proverb "Better late than never." Perhaps that procrastination to avoid bad company has been beneficial to my morality if to nothing else.

---

* English, Ananké — Destiny, fatality, force, compulsion, etc.

Here I begin to feel that my exordium to my discourse in relating the incidental anecdotes I have in stocks, is long enough and that I must come to facts.

In the period included between 187– and 188– I cannot be precise. I had one day the visit of two persons, whose external appearances looked to me as pertaining to the clerical profession; one of them especially, realizing my ideal of a Catholic priest in his outlines, that is to say from head to foot, in his all individual, dress, countenance, a rubicund — glossy — looking face, and with all that a sort of intellectual ———? I cannot very well find an adequate expression to define the thing, only, I fancied that there was something not genial a sort of *coarseness* in the whole, in the course of time I found that my suspicions were real, too much so, ten times under my approximation. You will be able to appreciate it when we come to the performance of the actor — *Artifex dolosus!* .... etc., etc., etc.

However he introduced himself as a man well posted with botanical technicalities, that which drew my attention, and he seemed to be aware of it. He conversed fairly enough, but his elocution did not seduce me, true, I was ill disposed to do him justice. I upbraided myself for being so prejudiced against him, but I could not help it.

In the long run of our intercourse I always studied his ways, manners, etc., in hopes to find something that would touch some chords of my heart, but I never found any thing but asperities, rough acting, and yet you could not strictly apply him those monkish rhymes —

"Mel in ore, verba lactis,
"Fel in corde, fraus in factis."

"Honey in his mouth, words of milk,
"Gall in his heart, and fraud in his acts."

"For he had no honey in his mouth, nor milk in his words,
"But he had surely *gall* in his heart and *fraud* in his acts *or actions.*"   L. M.

In spite of all my efforts I could not overcome certain feelings, not exactly of antipathy but not of sympathy as I understood it.

Nevertheless we looked all over the garden, greenhouses, etc. He knew good many plants and spoke knowingly about them, finally we parted and he asked me if he could come again. I told him he might come whenever he pleased.

Sometime after, I can't tell precisely how long, he came again with another person, he found me at the potting bench handling some Cacteacæ just imported, and almost before he had spoken a word to me he took one of the labels off one plant read it and told me: that! is not the name of a plant! it was a compound name of *two* greek roots, I told him the meaning of one of them, not knowing the other one at that time, and I told him next time you come I will tell you the other half of the name until then you have better go *to school* and *learn* before *teaching*. I gave him that advice in a pretty *rough way*, he felt it and I did not pay any more attention to him.

A number of years after he came again with an old acquaintance of mine. I thought they were two friends but they were not, the moment I looked at my Loyola I said here is my *teacher of names* but I was not materially sure, as it was a warm day and I knew my old acquaintance was a sort of aquatic plant, who could not stand long dry I went for some drink, I just discovered that my *chap* was more *or* as much fond of wine as of *holy water*, thus while drinking we began to talk with animation, while — I was analyzing him to convince myself that I was right, our conversation was waxing warm in exchanging some arguments of all sorts. I think I had just recounted an anecdote about a priest and a bishop, about Latin and drinking. Here is the story. A Bishop had company at his house and one priest of his diocese who was one of his guests, at breakfast the bishop had some wine he considered good and wished to know if his guests appreciated it. So he asked his priest a *connoisseur* in wine and also in Latin linguistic. Well, Mr. le

Curé! said the bishop, how do you like my wine? the priest answered briefly "*Bonus Vinum,*" "good wine." On that affirmation the bishop said to himself "My God!" I have a priest in my flock who is not very strong on Latin grammar, he does not know how to make agree a noun with an adjective and only two words! but he did not say anything before the company, in order not to mortify the priest before the whole society present, I shall question him apart. At the supper on the same day and the same company the bishop ordered the very best old wine he had in his cellar. When the time came to drink it our bishop asked again to his Curé, how do like this wine it is different of what we had at breakfast give me your opinion. He, the priest, rose from his chair and said emphatically his glass in his hand (he had tasted it before) "Monseigneur, Ecce Bonum Vinum!" to the health of the whole company! our bishop was — much surprised — confounded to hear his priests drinking his wine with so much enthusiasm and praising it *in good Latin,* he could not stand to wait longer, so he asked: Monsieur le Curé! Will you please tell me why this morning when I asked you how was my wine you said "*Bonus Vinum,*" and to-night you say "*Bonum Vinum*"?

He the priest answered coolly, "Bon vin, bon Latin" — good wine, good Latin.

(*Bon vin* and *bon Latin* rhyme in French.) This morning I have said *bonus* instead of *bonum* because the wine was of inferior quality, and to-night the wine being superior I say bonum, not bonus, just at that moment I was like the Bishop, I could not wait longer so I asked: Are you not the man who came to visit me many years ago? No, he said, Mr. Menand, I have never come to Albany or Troy before to-day! So in face of that affirmation I could not tell him he LIED, notwithstanding my moral convictions. We continued to drink and talk and I recounted the incident of "my Latin *Post scriptum*" I have related before in my recollections. Then he put his hand on my shoulder and said: "You! Mr. Menand! you—have—done such thing as destroying a letter of a priest. I answered that I had *done it* and *was proud of it*. His remark convinced me he was a priest, but not that he was the man who had visited me twice before. It was not a very long time after, that in a moment of *mental aberration*, for *Jesuits!* who seldom forget themselves, always on the lookout to *entrap* any body — *body* and *soul!* and more than *both* if you have it, *little* or *much* (money). This last article is equal to God in their religious statutes and dogmas. "Nervus belli pecunia," "Money is the nerve of war," whether you *wage* it, (war) to *nations* or to *consciences!* it does not matter as long as you can get what you aim at. It will be right if crowned by success.

> "Craftiness and shame from *all* conditions rise.
> "Act well your part, there all the *success** lies."
> — Parodied from Pope.

Night came and my visitors left, and nothing but empty bottles, but as a compensation my head full of fragments of conversation that were revolving in my brain as to suggest to me what I should do to elucidate the darkness of my ideas in reference to our visitors.

The following week one of the two (my old acquaintance) came and gave me explanations about their meetings, etc. Shortly after they came together again or separately, I am not positive — they were three, one, the third, was, I suppose, a companion — some *associate* of the young Loyola, as I have always understood Jesuits do, having *so much confidence* in each other's *uprightness*.... As customary with gardeners who always want to keep their *ideas damp* lest they should wilt.... I brought some wine, then, talk about plants, principles, morality, etc., etc. At once, as quick as lightning, our Loyola had a large clumsy-looking pipe in his hand and filling it with tobacco! Need I telling you that I felt somewhat *queer*, quirer! even a little mad! and I foresaw a coming storm but the flash

---

*Honor is of no account in priestcraft affairs!

produced, *lighted* my dormant philosophy and reason and instead of exploding one of my mental torpille (torpedo), it instantly made me *calm as a tomb* and waiting for *sensations*. I had not to wait long, in a few seconds our unceremonious follower of the worthy St. Ignatius was sat on a rocking-chair that was in one corner of our office communicating to a hot-house, and began to puff his not overfragrant tobacco smoke, whose stinking effluvia were going up to over a window in the top of which I had my "Motto ——

"Deus Nosque etiam nobis hac otia fecerunt."

"God and we also have given us this leisure"— English of above.

He sat directly *opposite* the *visual angle* where was the name of God!.... and seemingly enjoying seeing the smoke almost obscuring the name of God from reading. When, in a voice and diapason I shall not attempt to describe, not being a musician, I asked him if that motto in Latin and English was correct? He hardly took his pipe out of his mouth to tell me, he thought it was, and added "you have found — that —phrase— in—*some books!!*.... you hear! readers if any! but you cannot hear the *roaring of my soul*, in that moment, if I had not *contained* with all *my energy*, my *wrath* that man would not be alive to-day, and yet

I kept cool, relatively speaking, and having my heart burning. Then I told him "do you — think — if — during — all — my — life — time — I had — been — smoking — a — dirty — pipe — and — worse — tobacco, God would have given me *given us* these leisures we enjoyed in this very room?? he made no answer, but I continued my bitter-sweet *admonition* rather *caustic, burning* my heart: Ministers of God, if you will show me *any book* where you have seen this expression of my *veneration* to the supreme "Unknown" God! I will furnish you all your life-time with your dirty occupation, tobacco and wine also. Though it is not so many years that immoral incident happened, I cannot recollect the sequel, I think the whole party went away and that he never replied a word, dreading an explosion..

A long time elapsed before he came again, but he did that which I did not expect. Now I cannot help to think that many who may have read these lines I have written about such a man, and continuing an intercourse with him, may think I am not much more *dignified* than he was. I have said so myself more than once, yet his visits here continued sometime later, even after I had discovered his *lying to me*, when he said he had never come to Albany or Troy before that day he had confessed it to one of my sons by asking what had come of a certain plant he had seen *in such place* years ago, that he could not see it any where. My son knew nothing of it; he had never seen nor heard of the plant, besides, two of his friends came hither and told me that he had come hither many years ago and that they ought to visit me that they would see many things they would not see any where else. Now I must finish my confession, and that man's doings as a priest. He would not eat meat on a *Friday*, even on *Wednesday*. I once, without knowing what day it was, I offered him some *Italian dainty* called "Mortadella," some prepared ham — he would not eat it, because it was *Ash Wednesday*, yet he would not hesitate to lie any day in the week without scruple. However it is the *recollection* of that *circumstance* that brought our rupture for *ever*. I had very nearly taken him by the arm and shown him the gate of our grounds and tell him to clear as quick as he could walk but my reason, my philosophy, if you please, but *more than* that, my sudden remembrance of my long *shameful* intercourse with him prevented me kicking him out, for I found in my *conscience* I had been as wrong as he *was*, in my *tolerating* him, true, only on account of his being fond of plants, and that I could discuss linguistic with him. His ultramontane theories had become so intolerable that I made up my mind to turn him out in a gentlemanly way, that which I did. The last word I addressed him as he was going out with my maledictions, but *no* kicks (material) but some *mental ones* as *Jesuit! Tartuffe, Loyola! finis Æternum Vale!* — Adieu forever — Then he went off.

A few hours later when I went in the house I wrote to him a short but (accented) letter, in which, I told him — can't recollect the expression, but here is pretty nearly the sense....

I hope God will forgive me for having acted so long such a *shameful* part. You with your *coarse*, vulgar manners, hypocrisy, hellish Jesuitism, etc., and I with my complacent, stupid behavior listening to your sophisms like.... from this day all intercourses between us are at an end.... Finis Improbus!!

It is all over, wretch!!

AN ESSAY.

(Extract from the New York Horticultural Society's Report, 1883.)

By L. Menand.

Mr. J. Y. Murkland, Sec'y:

Dear Sir: — I regret much that the reading of the contents of the Philadelphia "Florist" has not convinced you that I ought to refrain from writing any thing on horticultural subjects for publication. You wish an essay on a special popular plant, the very thing I am incompetent to do, for many reasons. Firstly, I have no propensities to be an essayist, in general, and in particular on a specialty. I am no specialist, but, on the contrary, I am a *staunch eclectic* — therefore I could not confine myself to discuss on one subject alone. I would be very apt to jump from one to the other, and let my vein overflow my reason. And that you do not want. But supposing I could and should try to bind my mind to talk about one single topic — plant. What plant? All popular plants have been more or less ably treated. Roses, bulbs, ferns, orchids, etc. Nothing left but one of my hobbies, the *ostra-*

cised cacteæ, or other succulents, more, or equally insipid things to the æsthetic palates of your epicure philophytes!! lovers of plants and flowers, with wooden legs (stems) and other ornamental ligaments.

And these last are specialties, if any, especially the *cacti.* Yet, their protective spines would give us florists a good supply of *vegetable pins* to prop our floral productions. An essay on *our* Horticultural Society, that has been done. All I might do, and that which is more congenial to my feelings and turn of mind, would be to try a few digressions on what I think the best ways and means to promote the success of the society. But to elucidate one's ideas on such a *delicate theme,* and as *I understand it here, means:* improving the MORAL of the society and at the same time to teach how to grow the *"root of all evil"* and *good, too* (that PLANT ROOT belongs to my school, *eclecticism*) on a large scale. For, without that sine qua non, that nervus belli, that *universal panacea !* no success to be expected, and even with that somewhat doubtful to realize. For, before cultivating that *universally appreciated vegetable,* we must prepare the compost in which it will have the chance of thriving, without *bruising* the feelings of sensitive people. There is the stumbling-block to avoid. But, it strikes me that my preliminaries are getting lengthy enough. Shall I continue? If you answer affirmatively I *shall try —* "*mind*" I *don't say* I will, to be less confused and enigmatic in my narrative, and "If you choose that, then I am yours withal."

It occurs to *me* that before preparing the materials for the cultivation of our ROOT, it would not be out of place to recall to mind an episode — a reminiscence of a "*Horticultural Exhibition*," the first one I have attended in my life — in America — in Brooklyn, in 1840. I now forget the locality and even partly the plants exhibited. There were not many, but *passable*, even *good* for the time. Then, the *Camellia* and *Dahliomania*, fever *fanaticism*, which you may prefer, were reaching their paroxysm. It was a furor, a rage, as the *Orchidemy*, *Orchidomania*, epiphytal fanaticism of our days. Nothing was worth looking at but a newly grafted camellia, with one or two leaves, and occasionally a few more, or — *Dahlia* cutting, in three or four-inch pots, selling $1, $2, $3 to $20 apiece. We saw one plant (a dahlia), named Ne Plus Ultra, sold for twenty dollars to a gentleman still living in Boston. That Ne Plus Ultra was, and proved to be, a first-rate humbug. The possessor of that plant, Mr. George Thorburn, of New York city, had bought it in England for the moderate price £10, for one root. Does not that make a dahlia grower's mouth water!

After seeing the plant in bloom he ordered it to be thrown away. He did not wish to deceive anybody any more. By the way, the six best plants at the exhibition spoken above came from his place, Astoria. I only recollect the name of one: *Pimelea* decussata, a rare plant then, and perhaps rarer to-day. That plant found *warmer admirers* than wished for, for some one, *through distraction*, I suppose, took it away with another plant, and the year after he found both plants in Fulton Market, New York, and bought them again from a woman selling plants. The art of *prestidigitation* was already flourishing, and we think it has improved since that time. These digressions do not help me very materially in exposing my views on the means of *ameliorating* the elements of success of our Horticultural Society. The truth is that I don't know how to begin without *ruffling* the equanimity of our friends, if I have any; however, I live in hope to have some, even if I castigate "qui bene amat bene castigat."* I understand that we are going to have a new hall for our Horticultural Exhibition, without depending on anybody. This will be of *much more importance* to *success* than my *overdrawn phraseology*, but every one does what he can, *or thinks he does*. If so, *we gardeners, nurserymen, florists*, and all parties interested in horticultural affairs ought to understand each other when we meet at exhibitions, or elsewhere, not to keep

---

* Who loves well chastises well.

our *energies*, our *vital powers*, in *too much excitement*, in *too moist* an *atmosphere*, if I may use a *technical gardener's expression*, but *keep ourselves* as we do *orchids* when they have perfected their growth — *keep comparatively dry*, until the blooming season, then

. . . .

And above all, let us not indulge in *boasting* of what we *could have* done, and what we shall do, but *do it* to the best of our ability, and never tell any one: I *will beat you*, but if you chance to do it, *let us wait* until the defeated parties tell you so, and *we* will find it *much more gratifying* than self-praising, and if by chance, what may *very probably happen, we should* be disappointed with *potent reasons*, let us not show our displeasure, *if we can!* and swallow our mortification and prepare our energies for a new contest. *Mankind is not* infallible — judges, from want of knowledge or otherwise, *may err*, that is human.

One supreme recommendation I would propose. It is: as nine-tenths of us gardeners are foreigners, *Yankeefied Americanized, of course*, and assuming that in the *emergency we* would like to wrap ourselves in the folds of the star-spangled banner, and the eagle soaring over this immense continent, that *home to all of us, never say:* We have done *this* or *that* in the old country — at home, at *Lord's So-and-so*, but let us do it here, in this *earnest home*, not a home by *virtue* of a *short* or a *longer lease*, but by *virtue* of *liberty* and *industry*. Where liberty dwells there is our country!

One word more to the address of gentlemen's gardeners. *Do not indulge* too much in saying that your employer does not like or care for such and such plants, merely because you *do not like them* yourselves, and he has never told you so. He has got the plants and he pays you to take care of them, that is sufficient reason to do it. A man does not keep a gardener to do exactly what he likes. *He*, the proprietor, also wants something — some compensation for the money he pays, and for which sometimes he does not get *one cent* of satisfaction for *hundreds* of dollars spent. I speak *ex cathedra* — from *experience*.

It is not very long since I heard a certain chap say he wished such *rubbish, plants* he did not like — were on or under the manure heap, that he could not bear their sight, and would be glad to see *them all dead*. And he has in a measure acted accordingly. There would not have been so much harm if he had *taken good care* of those he *did not dislike* and his employer *cared for*, but they were all treated alike. To kill a plant, a *palm*, an Araucaria, or such, because they do not bloom in winter, to cut flowers from, or such irrational remarks, is about as sensible as if the possessor of a fine picture *threw it away* because the personages represented in it *do not speak!* In another instance I have heard one of those *planticide* gardeners, in presence of his employer, who had just bought an orchid in bloom, that he was lovingly carrying on his arm when he passed the remark, in looking at a Pimelea Hendersoni he also wanted to buy: "If *I buy* them, that fellow," pointing to the gardener, "will kill it! He will kill them!" To that remark the *planticide* replied quietly: "I would rather have a plant to which I could apply my *knife* than that *Pimelea* and Orchid." It seemed that man preferred to apply a *knife* to a plant than his *skill*. But likely he had the former and did not possess the latter, and did not care to. However that man had the courage to express his opinion in a very frank manner. It appeared to me that he had some good qualifications, for when he had killed a number of plants, his employer said that he would readily dig up a hole to bury them, or if in winter and the ground was frozen too much he would resort to cremation.

Having had the presumption to give friendly hints to my *confreres*, I feel the velleité — the temptation of offering some to *gentlemen keeping gardeners*, and on the "*ground*" that I have occasionally heard some of the former expressing their desire of cultivating certain plants — *orchids*, for instance, but that they only had one greenhouse or hothouse, and not a *special one*, as required for orchids, at least their gardeners said so, and they seemed to believe it themselves, and especially when they *may have heard* that half a dozen houses are necessary to grow with success that family of plants. Orchids — well? it *may be*, after all, that I am wrong, and that a series of such *plant dwellings* would greatly facilitate their cultivation. But how many lovers of those plants CAN and *would* afford the means to do it on THAT LINE? Very few, indeed. I, for *one*. I would be scared, even if I had the means to do it. Six houses exclusively for *orchids*, without the *admixture* of other plants! That gives me *chills!* — fits of "cacoethes loquendi" — itching — of talking — of expressing my opinions, as our friend the *planticide*, spoken above. Why should I not express my *Yankee notions* or *Yankeefied ideas*, as well as any one? Well! if this *privilege*, no! *right!* is granted to me, *I here*, emphatically and with all my *profound convictions based* on a little experience, and with all *due regard* and *deference* to all parties, including the elucubrations of theorists on that specialty, I *affirm*, I *maintain*, that *orchids can* be cultivated in *a mixed* collection of plants — tropical or others. Of course, tropical orchids with miscellaneous tropical plants, and so on, for all categories of plants. And if any one imbued with the contrary idea will pay me a visit I shall try to convince him, or them, of their error, *not in idle talk*, in which *I perhaps indulge too much*, but by and with *material facts*.

I have said that orchids can be grown in a mixed collection of plants and (if no other way of heating) *heated with the old antiquated flue system* (if *properly constructed*). *Old fogyism*, I fancy I hear some one murmur. OLD! *I admit it*, no matter what *sympathy* I may cherish for old things. I *don't recommend* it. But I say that with *a little good will*, a *little more brain* and *intellectual oil*, and, *above all, not depending too much* on *biped machines* — on your *assistants**— on your *men*, but try to be *men yourselves* — to be the "deus ex* machinâ," and you will find the machinery will run smoothly enough, abstraction of unforeseen accidents, of course.

Here I was to close my verbiage, when a sudden idea seizes me, reminds me that I must follow the undulating current of my conceptions and fill up the sort of *hiatus, chasm* in my above digressions. My *mere* affirmations that orchids may be grown in *a mixed collection* of plants, etc., is too *loose*, too *indefinite* to convince people who *think for themselves*. I feel I must explain myself in a more explicit manner. We

---

* The main spring of the machine.

have been told that half a dozen or so of different *structures* are necessary to cultivate orchids successfully. This number of residences for one single family of plants seems to me too extravagnant, too lavish. The mere enumeration of the names of those dwellings *congeals* the blood of my, *perhaps*, overheated understanding, as much *so* as *do* the long lists of *florists' flowers*, myriads of *unmeaning* names to *fill up* catalogues of "*capita mortua*," *dead-heads*, or next to; a difference in *names* and *prices only*, *a catch-penny trap*. I think I will be liberal, generous, in allowing this *aristocratic family of plants three* residences (*unless* it should be *composed* of *many generations* — in that case it would require more room), *and on one condition* — that *it* will *live in peace* with other heterogeneous families, such as *Crotons, Dracænas*, etc., etc. — a *hot-house* for Phalœnopsis Vandas, Angræcum and congeners, kept as recommended — minimum heat by night in winter, 60, 65. A few degrees, more or less, will not hurt any thing, unless it should be the *notions* of some horticulturists; but this *will not injure* the plants *if well taken care of*. One intermediate house (with the same reserves as above, *sociability* with each other) kept 50, 55, 60. This sort of *half-way* house will answer for *resting* or *retarding* some plants, if not kept *too moist* . . . . And one cool house, *i. e.,* that you will keep as cool as you will be able to do it, from June to September. This last REFUGE, will not require more than 40 degrees in winter (and occasionally less); a few degrees less will do no harm. In this house *we have had* some *few degrees below freezing point* for a *few hours*, and Cypripediums and Cælogyne cristata were not hurt. But *we wish* to be *understood* that we *do not advocate* the practice *to let the frost* in the house.

I shall not go into more particulars about the management of orchids or other plants, because I suppose that any moderately intelligent gardener knows the A B C of cultivation of plants in pots, etc. I do not suppose they need to be instructed how to *sharp their knives* when paring cuttings, or how to arrange *draining materials* in a pot, etc. These *stereotyped, silly dictums* can be found *in all* elementary *Books on Horticulture.* But I would like to bring to the attention of every one — the SACRED as well as the *profane* — the facts or *sentences* mentioned in the "Essay on Orchids." "*That in many instances the proper treatment of plants (orchids) and others, I suppose, has been arrived at* by '*accident*' — *chance.*" *Potent words to be pondered on,* as well by *professors, theorists,* as by students and learners of all classes. To study, to analyze, if possible, the *causes of accidents* and *failures,* as well as those of *successes,* and compare the former with the latter, and then, by synthesis, try to frame what you know of *practice* and *theory* in a sort of vade-mecum, to guide you in dayly? (or daily?) routine, and *not* say, "*It does not or will not pay.*" For, how do you know if it will or not without you try? You might say you have heard men of business say so, or that you guess. It is very well to guess, but it is much better to be *certain*. Besides, one may fail in an undertaking while another will succeed. Since some twenty-five years or more my brain feels sore from the frequent concussions of that phrase, "It does not pay"—words that *most* of the time have no more meaning than a "How do you do" exchanged between parties who care as much for each other as all of us care for *Buddha* or *Buddhism*. An acquaintance of mine has often thrust that *saying* in my face with the remark, that if I had done so and so, as he had done, I suppose, I would be much better off, etc. · · · According to that principle, the one who HAS NEVER DONE any thing but what *pays*, and another who has ALWAYS done what *does not*, it would follow that the *former* ought to be *better off* than the latter; that which I have not been able to see yet, although I have observed with a MORAL MAGNIFYING *glass;* but probably my sight is not like that of a great many people, who can see *an atom* in their neighbor's eye. Now, my friends, if I was not afraid to have already *abused* the privilege of talking beyond the limits of reason, I would like to tell you some little stories that have some *little* connections with the cultivation of the evil's root. You will see, if you allow me to go on. It may possibly edify you. *I have always, and I have not done* what *does not pay or pays*. But the truth is, that I have for the last *half century* spent many *days, weeks, months*, one, two, three, ten, twenty-five and thirty years in growing *plants, in rearing*, besides plants (some *intellectual notions* and a number of *other things* that *need not* be described here), that have taken me two, three, five, twenty, twenty-five years to *raise a customer to buy them*. As to the other *notions*, they have not been raised in view of making money, for I was convinced beforehand that all the benefit I would derive would be some *moral* gratification ; but, since, I have made *retrospective reflections*, that the best paying of the two was the "*not paying undertaking ;*" and DO NOT BELIEVE this a PARADOX, but A POTENT TRUTH.

And, if you please, I will exhibit some facts to corroborate what I have said. At the time the Brooklyn's Hort. Society was *flourishing* — thanks to the zeal of the President, Mr. Degraw — not to the gardeners, who, *partially*, with the *breaking out of the war*, 1860, *knocked it out of existence*, about 1855 or 1856, I forget, I exhibited some few plants. Among them were some large Polygalas and Laurustinus, etc. One of the last was a plant some 7 to 8 feet high, with *its tub*, and a stem perhaps 3 *feet high*, and of the diameter of a spade's handle, and the head 20 to 21, or perhaps 22 *feet in circumference*, with flowers enough to totally eclipse the foliage. That plant I had COAXED for about fifteen or sixteen years. By the way, I forget to tell the variety. It was Viburnum *nitidum*, whose foliage and flowers, when well grown, are about *double* the size of *tinus*, which is "*a good plant*," *notwithstanding* the declamations of some *moral, invalid, gardeners*, who *wittily* say it is *played out, used up, it does not flower*, which *is about right ;* but whose fault *is it*, the plant or the gardener? *I incline* to the *latter*. *Poor excuse*, when a plant does not do well to say that it is *a bad plant*. Why not say "*a bad gardener*," as *I do whenever I fail*. I do not know if *Nature* has created bad plants, but I am *pretty certain* she has in her *evolutions* produced men with very *weak minds*. *Excuse me this overflow*, and I come to our topic. A gentleman in Broolyn fell in love with that plant, and asked me if I would sell it. I answered affirmatively. Then he inquired the price. I told him $100. He said he would take it, and he thought that I could afford to give him a couple of *Ixora Coecinea* into the bargain, *which I did*. On hearing the result of the transaction, a *know-*

ing embryo gardener passed the remark that in England one could get a Laurustinus for *two-and-six* and *three-and-sixpence apiece*. I heard some one asking *him* if they were of that size. Oh! no, but they *would* grow *to that size*. When I left Albany with that plant I had four or five more large ones — two Polygalas and two Laurustinus, but of inferior size. A gentleman of Albany who saw them on board the steamboat told me, "Mr. Menand, if nobody in Brooklyn or New York has sense enough to buy those plants, when they come back to Albany, *I want them*." He saw them again on our wagon, coming home. He stopped the *men*, and told them to bring the plants to his house, that he *had bought* them before they went to Brooklyn. They did not mind, as I had not given any orders to that effect. In less than twenty-five minutes he was with me, and told me he wanted those plants that *I did not care* much to sell, although I *wanted the money* as much as he wanted the plants. He added, "*I do not ask you* how much you want, but *I must have them*." I think I got $140 or $150, I forget now. Was not that cultivating the *root?* And every year since that time up to to-day I have sold *contemporaries* of those plants, and I think it *has paid*.

. . . However, successful as I may have been, I would *not* advise any one to follow my example in raising such plants *alone*, as I have done, and in view of *making money only*. But, IF you want, if you wish and feel like *growing*, *cultivating both* the "*utile dulcis*," the *useful* and the *agreeable*, two very different *crops* — one the *crop-food* for the *body*, and the other crop for the *mind, the moral* — then I say *Go ahead! Forward!! En avant!! Help yourselves* and heaven will help you!

I have *in store* many more remarks more or less *edifying*, or perchance *soporiferous;* but discretion forbids me to say any more — sat prata biberunt. . . You have listened long enough.

Wishing *all* the members of our Horticultural Society, all *who love* Nature in all her various aspects, the fields,* the woods, even Orchids, for I am not *exclusive*, I am a sort of *pantophile* in the *vegetable kingdom's* LINE *understood!*

Au plaisir de vous revoir!

ALBANY, *January* 1, 1883.   L. MENAND.

---

* Qui fait aimer les champs fait aimer *la vertu* (Delille).
* He who inspires the love of nature inspires the love of virtue.

As it has been so often observed to me that my name is an *odd, queer* name, that I think it necessary to elucidate it, though it is as plain English as fluid, as limpid as the light of the sun when it shines. It is so much plain English that one cannot utter but very few words without using half of it, and the *tail* of it too.

An anecdote about that *transparent* obscurity (etymological): The first time I had the observation made to me on that — my — name, it was by a cadet from *West Point Academy* or *Polytechnic School.* I told him it was *all English!* He said he could not see any English in it. Then as I had to do with a *scholar* and a young man of twenty at least, I tried to explain the *enigma* grammatically: Cut or divide the name in two parts and read it you will have the word *men* plural of *man,* homo, vir! *sometimes!* then — *and, et,* a conjunction without which you cannot connect y ur expressions, sentences, etc.

He *looked* and *stared* at me, with his mouth half opened, but never spoke a word. Whether he understood me or not I cannot tell. Yet the man *appeared* to be an intelligent man probably with some *restrictions* as all *appearances* are apt to be, in linguistic, honor, probity, morality, etc., etc. Subject to interpretation....

A PROLOGUE BEFORE THE PERFORMANCE.
AN EPITHALAMIUM.

My Friends, — Our Friends.

There is to-day exactly half a century
We have been bound with the chains of matrimony.
My good half? oft has said with verity,
These chains though indissoluble to eternity
Seem light enough, even pleasant to wear!
For her, I dare say, they are gold ware,
But for the other party, who drags the fetters?
Don't you think his lot might have been better
Than to have been more or less, for years,
Obliged to listen to her would-be fears,
Of leaving too numerous a posterity;
Which, after all, is less than that Adam had the priority.

P. S.

Here: I intended to say nothing more of my tribulations,
Although I have many more in my recollections,
Therefore, I will close my narration, fear of being checked
For divulging that I have often been *henpecked!*
Henpecked, have I said? this is a hard word, I think,
Even when used jocosely, but when written with ink
It seems outrageous, if one considers that indiscretions
May have been the cause of the above castigation;
However, such is a long usage of subjection,
That I am *willing* to submit to a repetition
Of . . . .
        So let us rivet the chains again.

                              L. M. Oct. 31, '90.

NOTE ON "EPITHALAMIUM."

The enclosed lines have been written some two or three years, more or less, I cannot tell exactly; in idle moments, in the long evenings in winter time — at the time my wife began to talk about celebrating our Golden Wedding. I had only shown them to her a few days before she died. She read them twice and said "that suits me" I will get the document copied in *plain* handwriting, then....I passed the remark, what then? She answered me: You shall know it in time. A few days after I received a proof copy, with the *additions suggested* by HER, of the *allegoric Chains*, which I had forgotten or rather not thought of. She was much excited with the idea presenting a copy to every one she should invite, but she was especially so, *"to comment"* the *point of doubt* affixed to the words *"my good half?"* to prove she was and had been *good* without a ? but with *! ! !*. Alas ! ! she has not; destiny, fate, had decreed it should not be.

By sending the above document I fulfill her *desire* and also mine. *A desire much embittered.....*

L. M.

MEMORIAL

"Thou know'st 'tis common, all that live must die,
Passing through nature to eternity."

"At death we enter on eternity."
So Adieu! adieu! for ever!
Adieu! adieu! pour toujours!

A broken soul
Une âme brisée.

L. M. to A. M., Oct. 17, '90.

ADELAIDE JACKSON MENAND.

October 15, 1890.

Not in the freshness of life's early morn,
When hope was high and fair life's pathway shone
With promise of bright days to be,
A golden glory of futurity —
                  Not then the summons came.

Not when the noonday sun was high o'erhead,
When summer days fast to the autumn sped,
When from the hurry of youth's flying feet
The rest of noon was to the spirit sweet —
                  Not then the summons came.

Years had rolled on and brought that sweet repose
Which, duties well performed, the spirit knows;
Peace, rest and freedom from earth's anxious care —
Age only brought, with crown of silvery hair
                  And still no summons came.

Yet, all unseen by us, her nature grew
Nearer to heaven — our spirits never knew
How thin the veil concealing from her sight
The golden portals bathed in heaven's blest light.
                  Nor heard the summons come.

She heard, — the veil was lifted, all around
Flowed pleace eternal, — not a sigh — no sound,
No pain — no fear — no anguish — earth was gone
And to the raptured soul its heaven was born
                  When the blest summons came.

No tears — no fears — let every grief be stilled —
Why weep for her, who every task fulfilled,
Goes to her rest? pray rather thus may be
Life's blissful close for us — for thee — for me —
                  When the last summons comes.

Pará, *December*, 1890.   Edward S. Rand, Jr.

"REMINISCENCES"!!
1878.

ALBANY, N. Y., United States of North America, January 25, 1878.
To the Citizen VICTOR HUGO, Paris.
Sir! or Citizen!
        I know not how to address you to be heard from the *obscure station* where I am, to attain the *summit!* where you are. It is half a century (there are forty years I have left France, and I should not hurry to visit her, were it not that the *Republic* begins to *shine* there, though with a very *dim light*, just bright enough to read the name of the thing) that your name sounds in my ear, and when it is not the name, it is the *vibration*, that induces me to write you to ask you a great favor for me, for *us*, I and my wife, species of Philemon and Baucis, intend to visit the *Urbs* par excellence, Paris. When there, *we* wish to press the *hand* that has written the chapter ("in the Misérables") "*Une Lumière Inconnue*" "*An Unknown Light*," and very many things besides, "*Gauvin! and Cimourdain!*"— 93, !!! etc., etc. I hardly hope that you will answer us. At all events, permit us, at least in *imagination*, to press your hand with *our hearts united.*
                Your sincere admirers,
                    L. MENAND AND A. MENAND.

                          ALBANY, March 15, 1878.
To Citizen VICTOR HUGO.
        Thanks! many thanks! our project to visit France, Paris, this year shall be *realized* since you have decided it, by your answer. I was afraid you had taken me for a hunter of autographs, it was not that, nevertheless I am *very proud* to have it in such a circumstance.
    We shall not abuse of your time; just one minute to shake your hand and to receive a cast of your *flame!* and our desires shall be accomplished.   Yours sincerely,
                                L. M.

THIS FAC SIMILE IS THE AUTOGRAPH LETTER OF VICTOR HUGO TO L. MENAND, WRITTEN 22 FEBRUARY, 1878.

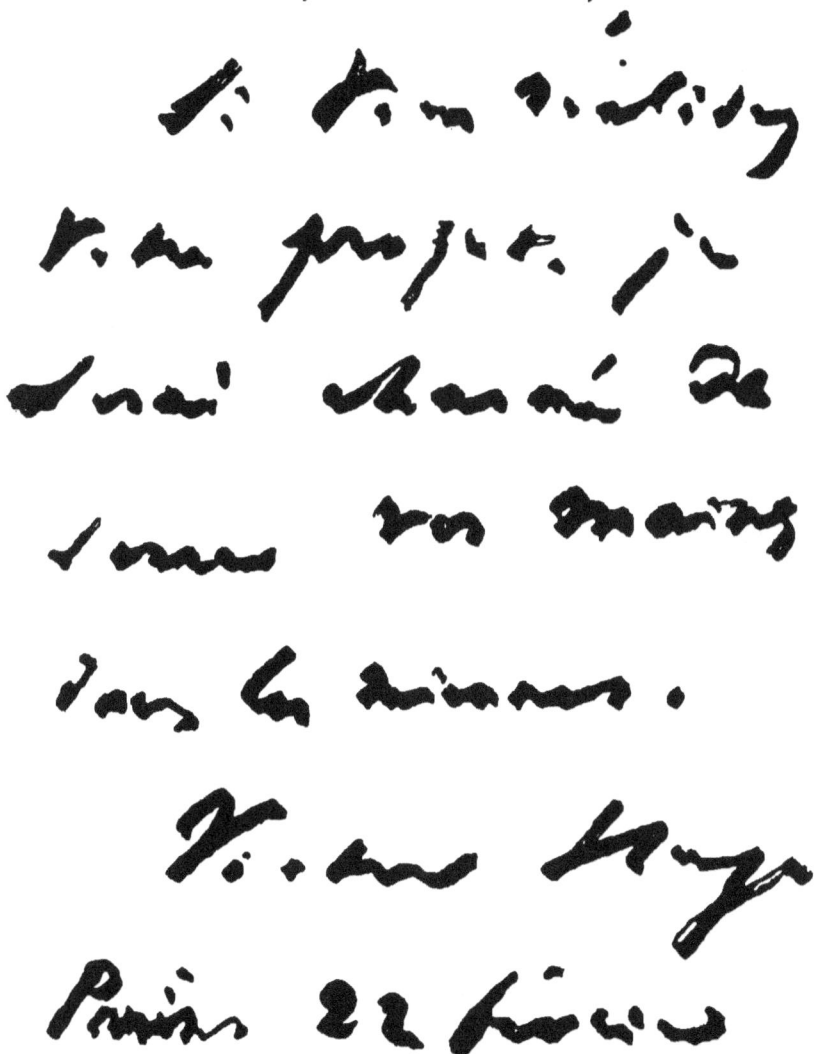

Si vous réalisez votre projet, je serai charmé de serrer vos mains dans les miennes.

PARIS, 22 *février*.　　　　　　　　　　VICTOR HUGO.

If you realize your project, I shall be charmed to press your hand in mine.

PARIS, 22 *February*.　　　　　　　　　　VICTOR HUGO.

Victor Hugo [signature]

"Reminiscences."

ALBANY, October, 1878.

To Citizen VICTOR HUGO. A *Whim!* on my return from France.

Veni, Vidi, Vici.

Veni! Oh ! yes ! I have surely come to see you,
But the *Vidi* has *lied* I did not see you,*
And the most mortifying of my deception
Is that, I shall never have such an occasion.
As to the *Vici* 'tis a word too elastic,
Which reminds me of a certain faith catholic,
However, I have conquered, the deep conviction,
That no matter what *shines* in any *old* nation,
And any where, beyond the Atlantic,
Is *less* fit to make a philosopher than a sceptic.
I close, begging you to excuse a semi-Vandal,
Who dares to address himself to the modern Juvenal.

P. S. Always more and more — Philèmon less the faith in Jupiter.

L. M.

---

* He had gone to Jersey not to return till November.

LOUIS MENAND.
1807 — August 2 — 1877.

I.
The golden light of August beamed
  O'er fair Burgundian hills,
The farewell glow of summer streamed
  O'er meadow, woods and rills.
The fruit blushed warm beneath her touch,
  Grapes felt the mellow glow,
Kind nature gave with lavish hand,
  'Twas seventy years ago.

II.
There, just as sombre night withdrew
  Before the golden morn,
As the first sun beams drank the dew
  A little child was born.
Fair nature bent above his bed
  A loving sponsor, kind,
To claim the infant for her own,
  To guide the dawning mind.

III.
She gently led him by the hand
  Thro' valley, field and wood,
Told how the secrets of the flowers
  Are known and understood.
From when the violets of the spring
  Bloom in the year's young day,
Till the pale Christmas roses beg
  The shortening days to stay.

IV.
She opened wide her secret books,
  And in his boyhood's hours,
He, eager scholar, learned by heart
  The lessons of the flowers.

Louis Menand.

Made them his loved, his bosom friends
    Friends that the dearer grow,
As years roll on; loved now far more
    Than seventy years ago.

V.

For him, were not life's crowded marts
    The din without surcease
Of noisy camp, but nobler far
    The gentle arts of peace.

*   *   *   *   *   *   *

Adieu, adieu, fair sunny France,
    Home of his boyhood's day!
Where the Atlantic's billows dance,
    The man pursues his way.

VI.

To the new land beyond its tide
    The wandering feet have come,
And where fair Hudson's waters glide,
    Content he finds a home.
Content for nature still his friend,
    Yields her abundant store;
There, as his years roll calmly on,
    He knows and loves her more.

VII.

Rich blessings spring around his path,
    And as his locks grow white,
After the heat and toil of day
    Life's afternoon is bright!
God grant him, in His own good time,
    When comes the close of day;
To the fair calm of starry night
    His life may melt away.

VIII.

That, in the garden of our God,
    Where flowers never fade,
Where nought that harms, has ever trod,
    Where none can make afraid;
Where welcoming angels shall entwine
    Immortelles for the brow,
My friends, may we all meet him there
    Say seventy years from now!

                            Edward S. Rand, Jr.

www.ingramcontent.com/pod-product-compliance
Lightning Source LLC
Chambersburg PA
CBHW020823230426
43666CB00007B/1072